THE CLEVELAND BROWNS
ALL-TIME ALL-STARS

THE CLEVELAND BROWNS ALL-TIME ALL-STARS

THE BEST PLAYERS AT EACH POSITION FOR THE BROWNS

ROGER GORDON

LYONS
PRESS

Essex, Connecticut

An imprint of Globe Pequot, the trade division of
The Rowman & Littlefield Publishing Group, Inc.
4501 Forbes Blvd., Ste. 200
Lanham, MD 20706
LyonsPress.com

Distributed by NATIONAL BOOK NETWORK

British Library Cataloguing in Publication Information available

Library of Congress Cataloging-in-Publication Data

Names: Gordon, Roger author.
Title: The Cleveland Browns all-time all-stars : the best players at each
    position for the Browns / Roger Gordon.
Description: Essex, Connecticut : Lyons Press, [2022] | Series: All-time
    all-stars series | Includes bibliographical references.
Identifiers: LCCN 2022026693 (print) | LCCN 2022026694 (ebook) | ISBN
    9781493066957 (paperback) | ISBN 9781493070749 (epub)
Subjects: LCSH: Cleveland Browns (Football team : 1946-1995)—History. |
    Cleveland Browns (Football team : 1999-)—History. | Football
    players—Ohio—Cleveland—Biography.
Classification: LCC GV956.C6 G664 2022 (print) | LCC GV956.C6 (ebook) |
    DDC 796.332/640977132—dc23/eng/20220705
LC record available at https://lccn.loc.gov/2022026693
LC ebook record available at https://lccn.loc.gov/2022026694

∞™ The paper used in this publication meets the minimum requirements of American National Standard for Information Sciences—Permanence of Paper for Printed
Library Materials, ANSI/NISO Z39.48-1992.

CONTENTS

INTRODUCTION

As one of the oldest franchises in the National Football League, the Cleveland Browns have a rich history, marked by championships, individual player awards, and countless thrilling games. But for today's fan, recent decades have been marked mainly by disappointment. After all, the last time the franchise had back-to-back winning seasons was in 1988 and 1989!

My goal in writing *The Cleveland Browns All-Time All-Stars* is to introduce younger fans to the complete history of the Browns, and in doing so send a signal that better days are around the corner. (Just ask fans of the Boston Red Sox and Chicago Cubs.) I also want to remind fans of a certain age of the proud tradition of a team that had its very first season in 1946. I believe that the best way to do that is through its players.

There was Otto Graham leading Cleveland to 10 consecutive championship games, seven of them victories. There was Jim Brown powering his way—and shedding tackle after tackle—to a Hall of Fame career that included three MVP awards and three appearances in the NFL title game, one of which was a victory.

There were Gene Hickerson and Dick Schafrath blocking for Brown and Leroy Kelly. There was Brian Sipe performing his magic in quarterbacking the "Kardiac Kids." There was Bernie Kosar directing the Browns to the doorstep of the Super Bowl three times.

There have been many other great players in Browns history who have contributed mightily to some very good teams, including defensive players Bill Willis, Bernie Parrish, Jim Houston, and Clay Matthews.

There have been some great head coaches in Browns annals as well. Paul Brown was such a huge name in football circles in the state of Ohio, he not only was hired as Cleveland's first head coach, but the team was named after him!

The very first player Brown signed? Otto Graham. Not a bad start.

There was Blanton Collier, who was the last head coach to lead the Browns to an NFL championship. There was Marty Schottenheimer, who turned the team around but couldn't win the big one.

When I was approached by Lyons Press about authoring this book, I simply couldn't resist. However, it was quite a chore compiling the Browns' All-Time All-Star team. There were so many players from whom to choose. I am sure that there will be readers who disagree with some of my selections. That's not a bad thing, though. Arguing who the best wide receivers are, who the best offensive linemen are, who the best cornerbacks are, etc., is a blast.

Let the debates begin!

HEAD COACH

Paul Brown
Blanton Collier
Marty Schottenheimer

How can one possibly begin a chapter about the greatest head coaches in Browns history without mentioning Paul Brown? The Vince Lombardi Trophy may be named after the legendary Green Bay Packers' head coach, but the father of modern pro football is Brown, the iconic head coach of the Browns from 1946 to 1962. Brown is credited with numerous football innovations. He was the first coach to use game film to scout opponents, hire a full-time staff of assistants, and test players on their knowledge of a playbook. He invented the modern facemask, the messenger guard, the practice squad, and the draw play.

Brown, who was inducted into the Pro Football Hall of Fame in 1967, led Cleveland to 10 championship-game appearances in 10 years from 1946 to 1955, winning seven. He led the Browns to a title-game appearance in 1957 and a playoff against the New York Giants in 1958. Whereas most teams back then ran the ball the majority of the time, Brown used quarterback Otto Graham's incredible talents to bring forth the passing game and blitzkrieg opponents through the air.

In Brown's last four seasons as head coach, Cleveland had good records but not nearly as good as the team had produced earlier in his career. Some players felt the game was passing him

Paul Brown coaching his players during training camp on July 29, 1955
(JIM HANSEN/LIBRARY OF CONGRESS)

by. After a 7-6-1 mark in 1962, team owner Art Modell fired the living legend, replacing him with assistant coach Blanton Collier.

The promoting of Collier immediately paid dividends. The Browns improved to 10-4 in 1963, just a game behind the Eastern Conference champion Giants. Collier opened up the offense. Quarterback Frank Ryan's statistics improved as did fullback Jim Brown's stats, which drastically increased. Collier's 1964 Browns shocked the Baltimore Colts 27–0 for the franchise's last NFL championship. He led the team to three more title-game appearances—in 1965, 1968, and 1969, the last two in which the Browns were on the doorstep of the Super Bowl. Collier had a hearing problem, which caused him to retire after the 1970 season.

After several years of despair in the 1970s, the Browns hired longtime NFL assistant Sam Rutigliano as head coach soon after the 1977 season ended. He immediately gave Brian

Sipe his stamp of approval as his quarterback and also third-year player Mike Pruitt his stamp of approval as his fullback. The Browns improved from 6-8 in 1977 to 8-8 in 1978 and 9-7 in 1979, barely missing the playoffs the latter year. During the early part of the 1979 season, the Browns, due to numerous games going down to the wire, became known as the "Kardiac Kids." Ironically, the most memorable win that year was a rout, by a 26–7 count over the Dallas Cowboys—"America's Team"—in a rocking Cleveland Stadium on *Monday Night Football*, which improved the Browns' record to 4-0 for the first time since 1963. Rutigliano was voted AFC Coach of the Year by United Press International.

In 1980, the Browns lost their first two games. They were 2-3 after five weeks. A miracle win over the Green Bay Packers in Week 7 was the turning point of the season. Rutigliano's troops lost only two more games all year in finishing 11-5 and AFC Central Division champions for the first time in nine seasons. Just like the season before, it was a wild ride through the schedule with most games undecided until late in the game. Rutigliano, for the second straight season, was named UPI AFC Coach of the Year. Even though Sam's questionable judgment quite possibly cost the Browns the game in their 14–12 defeat to Oakland in the divisional playoffs, he could have been voted Coach of the Century to Browns fans. Although he called for Sipe to pass the ball—which turned into an interception on a play called "Red Right 88"—when a field goal would have likely won the game, Rutigliano was still loved and cherished by Browns fans. That's what happens when you lead an exciting team to a division title and a playoff berth for the first time in eight years.

Four years later, it was a completely different story for Rutigliano. Toward the end of a Week 6 loss to New England, he made another questionable call eerily similar to Red Right 88 that cost the Browns the game. Two weeks later, on October 22, the day after a 12–9 last-second loss to the lowly Bengals in Cincinnati dropped his team's record to 1-7, Rutigliano was fired by Modell. Sam was now singing the blues. He was no longer the toast of the town. Due to the what-have-you-done-for-me-lately mindset of most fans, Sam's pink slip was long overdue. His Browns had fallen on mainly hard times since Red Right 88.

Rutigliano's replacement was defensive coordinator Marty Schottenheimer. Schottenheimer, a former linebacker for the Bills and Patriots, took charge and changed the climate immediately. Whereas Rutigliano was more laid back and perhaps loyal to longtime players to a fault, Schottenheimer put his stamp on the team from the start. He was more businesslike than Sam. He purged players who weren't helping the team. He won four of eight games in the second half of that 1984 season. His Browns won the Central Division, albeit with an 8-8 record, the next year and came within an eyelash of hosting— yes, hosting—the AFC Championship Game. Two 1,000-yard rushers in Kevin Mack and Earnest Byner plus a stingy, hard-hitting defense were what that 1985 team was known for.

It was obvious that the Browns lacked the strong passing game that was needed to complement the running game. Quarterback Bernie Kosar was not being used like he should have been. Enter Lindy Infante as the offensive coordinator and, bang! The Browns offense exploded in 12-4 and 10-5 seasons in 1986 and 1987, respectively. Unfortunately, "The Drive" and "The Fumble," respectively, those years—two tight defeats to Denver in the AFC title game—denied the Browns Super Bowl berths. Even after Kosar was injured in the opening game of 1988 and missed about half the season with three other quarterbacks seeing action, Schottenheimer was still able to get the

Browns into the playoffs. Philosophical differences with Modell led to Schottenheimer's resignation after the season.

A young Bill Belichick came aboard with two Super Bowl rings to his credit as the New York Giants' defensive coordinator. He improved the Browns but did not take them to the playoffs until his fourth season in 1994. Expectations were high as the 1995 season approached, but a 3-1 start disintegrated into a 5-11 record amid news halfway through the schedule of the Browns' imminent relocation to Baltimore.

After three seasons without pro football, the city of Cleveland welcomed with open arms the new expansion Browns in 1999. Other than two winning records and a single playoff berth, the expansion Browns were the joke of the league with head coach after head coach after head coach from 1999 to 2019. The team finished 1-15 and 0-16, respectively, in 2016 and 2017.

With the hiring of longtime Vikings offensive assistant Kevin Stefanski in 2020 as head coach, the Browns seem to have finally made the right hire. In his very first season, he not only led the Browns to 11 wins and a postseason berth but also a playoff win against Pittsburgh, their longtime nemesis. Although he had a rough go of it in his second season as Browns boss, Stefanski seems to have what it takes to be a successful NFL head coach.

It is much too soon, however, to make Stefanski one of the candidates for all-time best Browns head coach. The three in the running are Brown, Collier, and Schottenheimer.

PAUL BROWN

To begin with, Paul Brown had the ability to assess a player and make a determination that that player would fit into his system. Of course, when you have a great system and the kind of outstanding players he had, that made a great combination.

"Paul was a great innovator and a master psychologist in that he was able to make each player feel he was the most important player on the team," said Bill Willis, mainly a middle guard for Cleveland from 1946 to 1953, in the December 2006 edition of the *Orange and Brown Report*. "If I, for example, didn't do my job and we lost a game, it wasn't Otto Graham's or Lou Rymkus's or Dub Jones's fault. It was my fault. The players constantly tried their level best to outperform our opponents. And we tried to outperform each other. [Paul] used to tell us that he never went out on the field to play a football game that he didn't think he could win. And he was able to instill that kind of confidence in his players."

"He left no stone unturned," said Mike McCormack, mainly a right offensive tackle for the Browns from 1954 to 1962, in the January 2005 *Bernie's Insiders*. "He brought so many innovations to the game. The playbook was the first one. Paul used to say that what you're doing are the three principles of learning. You hear it, you write it down, and then you go out and enact it."

According to Bob Dolgan, a sportswriter and sports columnist for the *Plain Dealer* in Cleveland for 45 years, Brown was the greatest coach in the history of the NFL. "He by leaps and bounds is the most revolutionary coach in pro football history," he said. "He would have very light workouts during the week so that the guys were fresh and ready to go on Sunday. People who came to the Browns from other teams were amazed at how light the workouts were. Everything was scheduled ... five minutes of this, 10 minutes of that, 15 minutes of that. ... Quarterbacks used to call the plays, but he called all the plays with the use of the messenger guards. He'd send in a new guard every play with a new play."

"I had the opportunity to be a messenger guard my rookie year, which gave me a chance to really learn the system," John

Wooten, mainly a Browns left guard from 1959 to 1967, said. "It gave me an opportunity to really learn football at that high level. I had such a great appreciation of the system that Paul Brown had."

If you are going to make a coaching Mount Rushmore for the NFL, Brown obviously should be up there. "To me, he's one of the four greatest NFL coaches of all time," said Ray Yannucci, who covered the Browns for the *Akron Beacon Journal* for several years and was the editor of *Browns News/Illustrated* from 1981 to 2001 [he was also the owner and publisher for many years]. "And he was an innovator. He probably dealt with analytics before anybody knew what analytics were in football. He was way ahead of his time."

"He was brilliant, of course," said Dan Coughlin, a sportswriter for the *Plain Dealer* from 1964 to 1982 and the *Cleveland Press* for a short time and a local television sports reporter since then. "He surrounded himself with some pretty bright people, which was how he operated."

Brown is considered to be the father of modern football for all the innovations he brought to the game, but one he has never been given credit for is speed. "He wanted guys who could move, guys who had quick feet," said Steve King, a Browns historian who covered the team for the *Medina County Gazette* and the *Chronicle-Telegram* in Elyria from 1990 to 2003 and who was employed by the Browns writing for their website for several years. "His first Browns teams had those kinds of players. They were quick, they were fast, very athletic. Look at Dante Lavelli. He'd been a great basketball player at Hudson High School. He played some minor league hockey. Otto Graham had been a great basketball player. Lou Groza, as a junior, led Martins Ferry High School to the state basketball championship. Bill Willis was a tremendous athlete. Brown out-prepared other teams, and his teams were more physical than them.

"You look at the lines that Brown built, guys like Dick Schafrath, Gene Hickerson, and John Wooten. All those guys were fast. They're running downfield and making blocks, clearing the path for Jim Brown. It was that type of fast, light-on-his-feet player that Paul Brown carried with him all the way to the end of his career, even down in Cincinnati. Brown also was the first to use the trap play, the radio in the helmet, the conditioning, the spread passing game of today. That all goes back to Paul Brown. He was not afraid to be innovative. There was a lot of Bill Belichick in Paul Brown—no-nonsense guy, didn't laugh and joke, was very serious. It was his team. When he made a decision, that's the way things were going to be. In 1952, Graham held out because Brown took about two or three thousand dollars off his contract because he thought he had a bad year. That's just who Brown was. He wasn't afraid to make a tough decision and stomp on some people's feet and do what was best for the team."

Brown was a man who had a very tight organization. He ruled.

"In fact, I liked the fact that he had a very tight organization because he kept a lot of politics among the players out of the game," said the great Jim Brown, a Cleveland fullback from 1957 to 1965. "As an individual, he dealt with fundamentals, he dealt with how you carried yourself on and off the field. He was a very strong, aloof individual who was a top football coach, no doubt about it, with championship teams."

When Paul Wiggin, mainly a Browns left defensive end from 1957 to 1967, joined the Browns, he was mesmerized by their living legend of a head coach.

"When we rookies got there the first day, Paul Brown sat us all down and gave us a speech," he recalled. "He spent the whole day with us. I was somebody who had studied to be a teacher—I'd wanted to teach and coach—and after that first day, I thought Paul Brown was the greatest teacher I'd ever been around. I still believe that."

"I thought it was a great, great privilege for me to play under Brown," said Wooten. "I had the opportunity to learn under such a great football mind. I think that anyone who has really studied the game all down through the ages will realize that Paul was way ahead of his time. The West Coast offense that you hear them talk about . . . that's Paul Brown, and Bill Walsh would be the first to tell you."

"Paul was a pretty tough guy, but he was very intelligent when it came to football," said Jim Ray Smith, who played mostly left guard for Cleveland from 1956 to 1962. "You look back and you say, 'What did Paul Brown give to football?' And you look at Don Shula, you look at Weeb Ewbank, you look at Chuck Noll, and you look at Bill Walsh. I went and heard Bill speak at a luncheon one time. I went up to him afterwards and introduced myself, and he said, 'Yeah, I know you.' I said, 'You sound just like Paul Brown,' and he said, 'Well, where do you think I got it? I coached under him for eight years in Cincinnati.' You look all over, and Paul Brown's footprint is there."

Many players, among them Jim Brown, believed toward the end of Paul Brown's career in Cleveland that the game was changing somewhat and that he became a little predictable.

"Art Modell ended up making a move," Jim Brown said, "which we players didn't really create, but he made this particular move and got rid of Paul and brought [assistant coach] Blanton [Collier] in. And, at the time, Blanton was a breath of fresh air because we had benefited from all of the other things in the past from Paul. And now we had an individual who was a father-type, a friend-type . . . that's not to say that Paul wasn't a decent human being, but he was totally different in his demeanor and the way that he ran his organization. But I think that in the beginning, it was good to have played under Paul because, as a rookie and a young player, I needed that kind of discipline, I needed an organization that was tight. The players were never in groups because everybody was afraid of Paul, and we had pretty good results. And so I had the experience of that kind of discipline, and once having that, I wanted to expand myself, just like a child, when he comes into your life, eventually he wants to participate in decisions that are made. So I had a good respect for both of them but, as I said, we needed to change to Blanton, I think, to go that extra mile and to win the world championship."

Ross Fichtner, mainly a safety for the Browns from 1960 to 1967, saw the situation a little differently. "There were a lot of guys who felt Paul didn't have the desire to win as much," he said. "I thought he was still a great coach. When Paul left, Blanton's mouth was moving, but it was all Paul Brown's words because they worked together for so long. If you didn't know Paul wasn't behind there pulling the strings and saying the words, whispering in his ears, you wouldn't have known the difference."

BLANTON COLLIER

Browns players were getting a little tired of Paul Brown's lack of flexibility when it came to play calling and the structure of the team. Blanton Collier was already respected by the players. He brought a mood change, and it translated out on to the field.

If you look at the 1963 Browns, Collier's first season as head coach, it was virtually the same roster as the 1962 team, Paul Brown's last year as head coach. Collier brought option blocking to the team, a blocking concept that wasn't as rigid. He gave Jim Brown and Ernie Green more opportunities to find holes because of the options the offensive linemen were given in their blocking assignments.

"I think maybe the word that would best describe what Collier brought was flexibility both on the field and the players knowing that they were a little more their own selves off the field," said Mike Peticca, who covered the Browns for the Associated Press from 1976 to 1989. "Collier was a great tactician offensively. He had that reputation. He was also known as a very nice man but had the necessary toughness to be an NFL head coach. I remember just how highly respected he was. I don't think the Browns had much dissension during those years, which is another credit to Collier."

"He followed a tough act in Paul Brown," said Mike McLain, who covered the Browns for the *Warren Tribune-Chronicle* from 1980 to 2015. "Obviously, he was well-respected even to this day. He more than held his own."

As if supplanting a legend wasn't hard enough, disaster struck as Collier had to mend the mental wounds created by three tragedies before he even coached his first game. Running back Ernie Davis, the 1961 Heisman Trophy winner whose speed and power helped him break most of Jim Brown's records at Syracuse University, was acquired in a trade with Washington. Unfortunately, Davis contracted leukemia and passed away on May 18, 1963. A little more than two weeks after Davis passed on, standout safety Don Fleming was electrocuted on a construction project in Florida. Some five months before, sixth-round draft pick Tom Bloom, Purdue's Most Valuable Player as a running back in 1962, was killed in an automobile accident. Bloom, who had hoped to win a spot in Cleveland's defensive backfield, was driving the car he purchased with the bonus money he received for signing with the Browns.

"That was about as bad of an offseason as a team has ever had at any level. I think a lot of guys would've crumbled, but Collier fought through it," Steve King said. "You lose three players before you even coach a game, and oh by the way, you're taking over for the guy for whom the team is named. Nobody faced more of a mountain to climb than Collier before he coached his first game in 1963."

Collier had a great skill for teaching and developing his players. Said Paul Warfield, a Browns wide receiver from 1964 to 1969 and in 1976 and 1977, "His communication with me was what I'd experienced from grade school through high school to the university level with individuals who were teachers teaching in specific areas to widen the experiences or the development educationally. Certainly from the academic side of it of people to widen their experiences through knowledge, through literature ... he just transposed that into professional football and football in general in that he saw his players, from my interpretation, as students, and he wanted us to really fully understand why we performed certain skills. Certainly, he was a fundamentalist, he really wanted us to have the ability to comprehend, to understand, why we did certain things, fundamental things, such as what was the best way to execute blocks, what was the best way to execute pass patterns, as far as my background was concerned.

"He was very much a part of the Cleveland Brown philosophy—teaching, developing, understanding how and why one did things and got the job done. He was a hallmark of the Cleveland Browns' success in those days. It certainly took a certain amount of toughness to play the game of football because it's a physical game. The players had to have an appreciation for really understanding how to execute blocks, how to execute tackling, how to execute the other fundamentals, how to have the discipline to do that over and over again for the various positions to enable the ball club to have success and for the individual to have success."

Collier's ability to communicate is what made him such a good coach. His style of coaching was not to reprimand, yell, scream, or use profanity. It was in the mold of classroom teaching and developing. "He had a way," Warfield continued, "that was very effective of communicating with one without yelling or screaming to make one understand that not only did you let the team down but you let yourself down because you did not have the discipline to do that. So his ability to communicate without going to what was considered to be some of the accepted methods to be effective . . . he was a conversationalist and a man who did not revert to the yelling, the screaming, or the profanity, whatever it was, to make men supposedly tougher."

According to King, had Collier not had his hearing problem, the early 1970s would have been much different for the Browns. "They would've been able to continue a lot of the success that they had," he said. "Collier was just a brilliant guy. He was like an updated version of Paul Brown when he took over. He had the toughness of Brown, but he also was a players' coach, was very compassionate. He wanted to engage the players in the formation of the game plan and wanted to pick their brains to see what they thought. Brown didn't do that. He said, 'This is the game plan, and here it is, guys.' There was no discussion on it. Collier went to the players and asked them, 'What plays do you like to run? What could we do here and there?' He was just a tremendous coach."

"Blanton was the best teacher I've ever been around," said Fred Hoaglin, who played center for the Browns from 1966 to 1972. "He could teach every single position in football, the fine points, the footwork, any of the techniques. He was really an awesome teacher. He was an awesome person, too. He was so positive. He was fun to be around because he was always thinking about how to make the team better. He was very serious about doing your job well. He pointed out what each player needed to do to do better and helped us work on it. He was very, very astute as a coach. He was the best at studying film, detecting ways to get better. He was as fine a coach as I've ever seen."

"I felt I could trust Blanton," said Dale Lindsey, a Browns linebacker from 1965 to 1972, in the August 2004 *Bernie's Insiders*. "He had principles and philosophy, and he didn't change them because the situation changed. That's a rarity, especially when money and egos are involved. If you were a great player and did something wrong, you were punished. If you were a bad player and did something wrong, you were punished too. If we didn't play well, he'd tell us in a nice manner, but strong and firm. And if he had to bench a player, he had no problem with that. He did it with [quarterback] Frank Ryan [for Bill Nelsen in 1968]. That was a pretty damn tough decision, and it may not have been a popular one."

"Blanton [rarely] said anything to me for nine years, and when he did, it was before a big game," remembered Gary Collins, a Browns wide receiver from 1962 to 1971, in the August 2004 *Bernie's Insiders*. "He would say, 'I need a big one from you.' And that's it. He never got on me. My entire career, I was used to coaches riding my ass, and now they found out that wasn't the only way to do things."

The Browns' 27–0 upset of the Baltimore Colts in the NFL championship game in 1964 will go down as Collier's finest hour.

"It's all about how you prepare and plan on Mondays and Tuesdays," said Dick Schafrath, a Browns left tackle from 1959 to 1971. "If you don't plan and prepare right in how your attitude is for the rest of the week, that'll show in how you perform on Sunday. It was preparation. And we knew on Monday when Blanton gave us that game plan and laid it out and said, 'Here's how we're gonna win,' we were sold, and boy, everybody was convinced that that was the way we were going to beat Baltimore, and there was no way that we wouldn't win."

"The week leading up to the game was the best I ever saw us practice," said Jim Kanicki, who played right defensive tackle for Cleveland from 1963 to 1969. "Everyone was ready to go when we got to the stadium on the day of the game. Blanton did a great job of getting us ready."

Kanicki remembered a quiet confidence in the locker room at halftime of the scoreless tie. "Blanton had that effect on you," he said. "He was more like a professor than the volatile head coaches like Vince Lombardi and so forth."

According to Ray Yannucci, Collier should be in the Browns' Ring of Honor. "He's probably one of the most unsung head coaches in NFL history," he said. "He has one of the best winning percentages of any coach in league history. He won the last NFL championship for the Cleveland Browns. If you look at his eight years as head coach of the Browns and look at Paul Brown's last eight years as head coach of the Browns, you'll see that Collier was far more successful. People say, 'Blanton won with Paul Brown's personnel.' Maybe the first year, but if you look at the years prior to that, Paul Brown was losing the team. A mutiny was starting with Jim Brown and some of the other players, especially the stars. That's basically why Art Modell fired him. So even though some of those players from the Paul Brown era were a residue into the Blanton Collier years, Collier took a team that was dramatically on the down slide. In two years, he took the Browns to the NFL championship. In two years! He deserves far more credit than he gets."

"Blanton was an outstanding teacher and person," said John Wooten.

"Not only was Blanton a technician in all areas of the game, he was a great man, a great gentleman, a great leader," said Billy Andrews, a Browns linebacker from 1967 to 1974.

"I really think," King added, "had he not had to retire because of the hearing problem, he'd be in the Hall of Fame."

MARTY SCHOTTENHEIMER

Marty Schottenheimer got his shot and took advantage of it—pronto. When he replaced Sam Rutigliano as head coach in 1984, the Browns immediately began playing better football.

"I think he was a great defensive coordinator," said Joe DeLamielleure, who played right guard for the Browns from 1980 to 1984. "And when he became the head coach, he adapted quickly. He was really smart, hardworking . . . he never left a stone unturned. He was always looking for an edge. He was a really great coach."

"Marty was very organized and detailed," said Doug Dieken, a Browns left offensive tackle from 1971 to 1984 and the color commentator on the team's radio broadcasts from 1985 to 2021. "He had his goal set to be a head coach. He did well with the defense and then went on and became a very successful head coach."

"I liked Marty," said Mike Pruitt, a Browns fullback from 1976 to 1984. "He was tough. He didn't take no stuff off of anybody. But he was fair. He did a great job with the defense before he took over for Sam. Before he got in there, our defense was a little suspect, but he turned it around. And him becoming a head coach was something I knew would probably happen to him."

Schottenheimer grew as a head coach, especially from the offensive standpoint. "You look at that 1985 playoff game at Miami, and the Browns just didn't have many options offensively," Mike Peticca said. "Once that game got close, once that 21–3 lead shrunk, and once they got behind, they didn't have many options. They were pretty predictable because the passing game was pretty primitive. So Marty grew in that regard, and of course, much credit has to go to Lindy Infante, who came in the next year as offensive coordinator and turned that around."

Schottenheimer was a strong, tough coach who also had mixed in there the right blend of compassion and understanding, having been a player for several years himself. He was never a star or a player who necessarily had even a roster spot clinched, but he was a hardnosed player and a respected player. He identified with those types of players well, and he utilized marginal players or the players with lesser roles very well. "I'm sure there's some unhappiness among some players on every team," said Peticca. "Every team has guys who aren't especially happy with their roles, but I think that was minimized as much as it could've been with the Browns under Schottenheimer. I think one reason those teams were very good was that the whole roster would be used. I think the roles of the players were pretty specific and consistent. Guys knew what was asked of them, and they basically produced."

"Schottenheimer was a great coach," said Steve King. "He got the Browns back to being disciplined and running the football when he took over for Sam. The players loved him, stood behind him. He had a keen eye for talent. He did a lot of great things. When you think about that run from '85-88 … four straight playoff berths, two trips to the AFC Championship Game, narrowly missing two Super Bowl appearances, three division titles. In '88, he did his best coaching job. They lose all those quarterbacks. That team was so good, and his ability to keep it afloat was so strong."

"Marty was a coach's coach," Mike McLain added. "He always said, 'Our goal is the Super Bowl and nothing else.' Why *wouldn't* that be your goal? He was a very good X's and O's guy. He's probably underrated as a motivator. A lot of people looked at him as a coordinator-type guy, but he turned out to be one of the better head coaches in Browns history."

"He made me the professional that I became," said Ozzie Newsome, a Browns tight end from 1978 to 1990. "He did not want me to be one-dimensional. He wanted me to be the complete player. He allowed me to be a leader for him."

"I think Marty was a great coach," said Jeff Schudel, who has covered the Browns for the *Lorain Morning Journal* and the *News-Herald* in Lake County since 1981. "What really struck me about him was the compassion he had for his players. Here's an example. Johnny Davis was a fullback for the Browns, and Marty had to cut him. Marty became so emotional about it that he cancelled practice that day."

Schottenheimer's stubbornness got him into trouble at times. "That's what got him fired [he actually resigned]," Ray Yannucci said. "He didn't want to listen to Art Modell about getting rid of his brother Kurt and also about getting an offensive coordinator. He was a very emotional guy. He would cry at the drop of a hat."

Marty Schottenheimer (JERRY COLI/DREAMSTIME.COM)

"He was stubborn to a fault, and that cost him the AFC Championship Game in 1986," said King. "He went into that prevent defense on that 98-yard drive. The Broncos didn't win that game as much as the Browns lost it."

Schudel pointed to something else that likely cost the Browns that Denver game. "You can't ignore the fact that Schottenheimer's playoff record wasn't very good, but there were circumstances beyond his control I think," he said. "Had Don Rogers not died of a drug overdose, the Browns probably would've beaten Denver in that game."

According to Peticca, Schottenheimer's successful win-loss record validates his approach. "Some people still question his style, saying it was a little too conservative at times," he said. "That may be true. Maybe there are reasons he never got to a Super Bowl, but there are also reasons that he had a great record and that so many of his teams were contenders. I think the guy needs to be credited for getting *to* the big games. When people say that he couldn't win the big game, well, you have to *win* big games to *get* to big games, and he won a lot of big games. His playoff record isn't great, but he kept teams playing, he got teams there, but they just came up short. I hope he goes into the Hall of Fame and think it would be justified."

AND THE WINNER IS . . .

Although his teams became a little lackluster toward the end of his time in Cleveland, one cannot deny the fact that Paul Brown built a dynasty, a team that played in 10 straight championship games from 1946 to 1955, the first four in the All-America Football Conference, winning seven of them. The Browns returned to the title game in 1957 and lost a playoff to the Giants the next year before the downward slide began. Brown's list of football innovations is seemingly endless.

When Art Modell fired Brown, it was big news, huge news. Here was a former advertising executive whose football know-how was not exactly George Halas–like letting go a man who was a living legend in Ohio football circles, and not just for his time with the Browns. Brown also had been the head coach at Ohio State University, leading the Buckeyes to the 1942 Associated Press National Championship. Before that, he was the head coach at football-crazy Massillon Washington High School, leading the Tigers to a .909 winning percentage and six consecutive state titles plus four National Championships.

Blanton Collier proved he was up to the giant task of replacing a living legend when he took over for Brown in 1963. In Collier's eight seasons at the Browns' helm, he had seven winning records, five postseason berths, four league-title game appearances, and one NFL championship. In only his second season as head coach, he led the Browns to the NFL title, still the last time the team was crowned champion. Had he coached a few more seasons, he very well might be in the Hall of Fame.

Marty Schottenheimer was a breath of fresh air that Browns fans needed. He took over a downtrodden team that had produced two losing records and a playoff team with a losing record in the previous three seasons. He turned the team around faster than anyone could have imagined. In just his first full season as head coach, the Browns won their division and nearly toppled heavy favorite Miami in the playoffs. In only his second and third full seasons, the Browns advanced to the AFC Championship Game, falling in consecutive heartbreaking contests to the Broncos. In his four full seasons as head coach, he produced four playoff teams and three division titles.

The envelope please? How can you vote against a coach who churned out championship-game appearances factory-style? How can you go against a man who, soon after becoming the Browns' head coach, said he wanted his team to be the New

York Yankees of pro football? And it darned well was. The head coach of our team is **Paul Brown**.

COACHES WHO DID NOT MAKE THE CUT

There has likely been no other head coach in Browns history who was loved by his players more than **Sam Rutigliano**.

"It was great playing for Sam because he was down to earth," said Mike Pruitt. "You could talk to Sam personally. He was always the type of guy who would listen, not try to tell you everything, but he would listen. Sometimes you just wanted to get things off your chest, and Sam was that kind of person."

"Sam was a players' coach," said Doug Dieken. "He was kind of loose. He always had his one-liners. He was a little bit more relaxed than his predecessor, Forrest Gregg."

Rutigliano had a special way of encouraging his players.

"Each player is different," he said. "You have to kind of know where that button is for each guy. I really believe that."

Even though he was an offensive-minded coach, Rutigliano had also been a secondary coach, so he knew a lot about that area. "That endeared him to me, knowing he could watch practice and see something that a guy was doing and come over and correct him and teach him," said Thom Darden, a Browns safety from 1972 to 1974 and 1976 to 1981. "He knew what the player was supposed to be doing, the steps he was supposed to take. So that was always a positive for me. He was a good teacher, and I enjoyed playing for a coach who taught."

"Who did not love Sam? I loved him," Dan Coughlin said. "The players loved him. Sam started the Inner Circle [a substance-abuse recovery program for Browns players]. He took care of people. He was just such a likeable man. When he got fired, he was the only coach in my following the Browns who showed up at his own press conference announcing him being fired. He was asked, 'Would you do anything different?'

He said, 'Yes, I would kick field goals.' He got in trouble a couple of times where he went for the first down instead of taking the easy three."

"We always think of Sam as a nice guy, and that's true," said Mike McLain. "When the Browns won the Central Division title in 1980 by beating Cincinnati, the fans were just packing the airport, so we had to go to another area where they couldn't mob us. It looked like the Beatles landing. I looked out the window and there are thousands of fans there. Sam and I were the last people to get off the plane. The guy who I replaced, whose name was Jim, had been pretty ill. Sam said to me, 'Stop by my office tomorrow. I've got a game ball I want to give to Jim.' Here he was, thinking about some sportswriter who is ill in Warren, Ohio. Sam was a great person. I don't ever remember a player who didn't have a good word to say about him."

Rutigliano also was a pretty darned good football coach.

"Sam's reputation, and I think justifiably so, is better than the record indicates," said Mike Peticca. "Forrest Gregg's last team in '77 had fallen apart, and there was a lot of unhappiness among the players with him. I think Sam in '78 immediately restored somewhat of a comfort zone to be a Browns player. He had a lot of empathy for situations, and I think that maybe goes back in part to the accident when he lost his daughter some years before he was with the Browns. I think that built a real empathy in him for players' situations. I think he was good at sticking with guys, giving them second chances, and I think everybody on the team appreciated that.

"Obviously, he was a creative coach from an offensive standpoint, and beginning in '78 through '80, got good production out of the offense. If you look at that offense, there were some really good players, but I think they got the most out of it that you could ask. I guess that offense scares you if you're an opposing defensive coordinator, but it may have been just a little short of the absolute best offense like the Chargers. Rutigliano and the offensive coaches got the most out of those guys as they could. I thought what those offenses did from '78 through '80 were a lot of credit to Rutigliano and his creativity."

According to Rutigliano, his 11 years as an assistant coach for four NFL teams were very beneficial. "Doing it around guys like Hank Stram, Lou Saban, and Weeb Ewbank, I learned a lot," he said. "I kept a diary of all the different things that I *wasn't* going to do and the different things that I *would* do if I ever became a head coach."

Two of Rutigliano's signature wins came during the 1979 season—a resounding 26–7 Monday night victory over the Dallas Cowboys that improved the Browns' record to 4-0 and, two months later, a 30–24 nail-biter in overtime against the Miami Dolphins that greatly enhanced the team's playoff chances. "We played very well that night against the Cowboys," he said. "The crowd, the Monday night, the Dallas Cowboys, Tom Landry ... Lou Groza said to me the next day in Berea, 'Boy, what a great feeling that must've been for you.' I said, 'It's inexplainable. It's inexplainable.' I would go into Art Modell's office after every home game, win or lose. Obviously, it was always better when you won. But after that Dallas game, he was just ... if we could've stopped right there, we would've both walked into the Hall of Fame in Canton, Ohio. It was great. I really cherish the moment."

The win over the Dolphins was Sam's "I really am in the NFL" moment. "Miami had the number one defense in the NFL," he said. "And that Saturday night the Browns' all-time team—all the famous players—came back and gathered at a hotel on the west side of town and were also at the game. Dante Lavelli, Lou Groza, Otto Graham ... and I'm there saying to myself, 'This can't be true, this can't be true. Here I was a kid watching these guys play, and now I'm here shaking hands with them, and I'm the head coach of the Cleveland Browns!' It was a great moment."

The season before, in Rutigliano's fourth game as a head coach and in a battle for first place, the Browns lost in overtime, 15–9, at Pittsburgh in an extremely controversial manner. "We were undefeated and they were undefeated," he said, "and we got screwed on the first play of overtime and lost the game. So I took the moment and said to the players after the game, 'Look, let's capture the moment. Now, listen to me because I'm only gonna talk for about two or three minutes. This is the best team in the world! And I want you to know that there are gonna be 10 or 12 players on that Steelers team who are gonna be enshrined in Canton, Ohio, about 25 years from now. Let's be able to understand what you did against this kind of a team.'"

Rutigliano's legacy will always be the 1980 season in which the Browns unseated the six-time defending AFC Central Division champion Steelers.

"Sam choreographed it, and Brian Sipe was the trigger-man," said Steve King. "It was the most fun I've ever had watching any team in any sport in any season. It was a party every single Sunday. If you went to a producer and said, 'Let's make a movie about this,' they'd laugh at you. They'd say, 'That's too hokey. That doesn't happen in real life.' Well, it happened in that 1980 season. You'll never see anything like that again. Sam made that so much fun. He was the perfect guy for that. He got a lot of guys to play beyond their limits and brought out the best in all of those people. He developed a lot of guys and knew how to put the right person in the right place at the right time.

"His ability to communicate was his strength. He really knew how to wow the guys behind him. He had a good head for talent. He took Dave Logan and moved him from tight end to wide receiver. Logan was sputtering at tight end. Sam took a kid who had been a wide receiver at Alabama and put him at tight end, and Ozzie Newsome was born. The tight end becomes more than just a player running seven yards downfield and catching a hook pattern. Newsome was too big for safeties to cover and too fast for linebackers to cover. Ozzie was the first of them. And Brian Sipe through the 1977 season had never really distinguished himself. It wasn't until Rutigliano came in and told him, 'You're my guy' after doing some studying on him. He put him in there and let him learn that offense."

The Browns' remarkable 1980 Kardiac Kids season came to a crashing halt in a 14–12 loss to Oakland in the divisional playoffs on a treacherous weather day in Cleveland. Rutigliano eschewed a field goal try by Don Cockroft and instead had Sipe attempt a pass on third down at the Raiders' 13 yard line with 49 seconds left. The pass was picked off.

"The field was a sheet of ice," said Rutigliano. "I've never been more respectful of football players than I was that day, with what they had to go through. I mean, there were icicles in their noses. Brian just threw a bad pass, that's all."

After that memorable season, things fell apart.

"The problem was, Sam started trying to save lives with that Inner Circle when the Browns got hit with that drug epidemic," Ray Yannucci said. "I think that took away a lot from his coaching, and he started to make some bad hires on his staff. If he would've been able to last the '84 season, he would've taken Bernie Kosar to even higher levels than he went."

Seven years after Rutigliano was canned, Modell hired the head coach he thought would finally take the Browns to the Super Bowl. His name was **Bill Belichick**. In his very first meeting with his players, he made it known with a bang that he was in charge.

"It was a two-and-a-half-hour ordeal where he told us just exactly how crappy we were," said Mike Baab, a Browns center from 1982 to 1987 and in 1990 and 1991. "And then he finishes up by saying, 'I have worked too long and too hard to get where I'm at to let any one of you fuck it up for me. If you get in my way, I will crush you. Now get your asses outta here, I'll see you in the morning at 6 o'clock. And we all said, 'Oh my god!' We started calling our agents: 'How the hell do we get outta here?' And that was pretty much the tone of the entire Bill Belichick experience. Bill was about, at that time, the most unfriendly, unsociable . . . it was like he needed therapy."

The first year Belichick was in Cleveland, he met with everybody in the media. He told them what the ground rules were going to be during training camp. "We kind of walked away thinking, 'This guy's going to be pretty good to work with,'" said Mike McLain. "And then the first week of training camp, I asked a question about an injured player's status, and he just ripped me apart. I remember somebody coming up to me afterwards and saying, 'I'm glad you asked that question. We've got a good sound bite.' From that point on, we realized, 'This is not going to be your usual head coach. It's going to be confrontational.' He clearly was in over his head. It's hard to say that now since he's maybe the greatest coach in the history of the game."

"When he came in, he gave the impression that he was going to be a very, very open person to the media. He sat down with each member of the media individually," Yannucci recalled. "Well, he was not that kind of media-friendly coach. After his first season, he had a season-ending press conference and was absolutely fantastic. As he was walking back to his office, I stopped him and said, 'Bill, you were fantastic today. Why weren't you like that all year?' He said, 'Ray, I thought I was.' I said, 'Bill, you've got to be kidding me. You were the total opposite.' He was great one on one with reporters. He wasn't ready to be a head coach at that time, though."

On the other end of the spectrum, Belichick improved the Browns after inheriting a garbage team his first season. He offered glimpses of what was ahead of him in years to come.

"He was so far ahead of the curve that it looked odd," said King. "We didn't realize how smart he was. He was so different. He saw things that nobody else saw. He was so far ahead of his time, we thought he was crazy. He was *not* crazy, he was maybe just a little too far ahead of his time. I never saw a guy break down anything so meticulously as Bill Belichick. He had a great mind for football, he understood football. It was different. It was not fun like it was when Sam was there or when Marty was there with Kosar in the last half of the '80s. It was more of a businesslike approach. He brought that New York, down-to-business kind of style. He won in '94, and I think he would've continued to win had the announcement of the move to Baltimore not happened when it did. No one had ever been through anything like that. I don't blame all of those losses in the second half of the '95 season on Belichick. I don't care if your name was Brown, Lombardi, Shula . . . whoever you were . . . you were doomed to fail in that situation."

"Playing for Belichick was tough to say the least," said Kevin Mack, a Browns fullback from 1985 to 1993. "Bill was given all the power, and we were players. We had to do what we were being coached to do. And we were also getting paid to do it, so we had to do what the man wanted."

"Cutting Bernie Kosar is what he will be remembered for in Cleveland," said Jeff Schudel. "It turned out he was right about Kosar. His skills *were* diminishing. He didn't do a lot after that. Who knows what would've happened had the Browns not moved and stayed around? Belichick could've turned the Browns into what the Patriots became. You never know."

Fast forward to 2020, which, in Browns Town, was brimming with hope after decades of frustration. **Kevin Stefanski** was a major reason for that.

"I think what Kevin did in his first season was nothing short of remarkable," said McLain of the Browns' 11-5 season that also included a very satisfying playoff win at Pittsburgh. "The way he handled the whole COVID situation was amazing. He brought discipline to the team. They looked like a professional football team, which hadn't been the case for several years."

"I like Stefanski," said King. "The modern coach is a guy who is unflappable, and that is this guy's strength. I'm sure he's got a hard edge to him and probably has been animated in closed-door meetings with his players and assistant coaches, but he's unflappable. He doesn't get wired up about things. You see him on the sideline . . . he's like Paul Warfield. You looked at Warfield, you never knew whether he just caught a touchdown pass or dropped a pass, which was rare. He was unflappable. You couldn't get under his skin. And I look at Stefanski the same way. He doesn't get overly excited when things go well and not overly depressed when things don't go well. For him to be able to maintain his cool, I think, says a lot about him, and I think the players respect him for that. He's an unbelievable organizer, a planner. There could not have been a better hire than Kevin Stefanski.

"You look at Stefanski's first season and the things that happened. That playoff game in Pittsburgh . . . he couldn't go to the game because he had COVID, and there were some assistant coaches who couldn't be there. And the Browns go over there and just annihilate Pittsburgh. It was incredible! I think that's the structure Stefanski had built with the Browns. It was so dynamic that it existed even though he wasn't there. I think his ability to organize a plan, that he got the players to buy into it, and then stuck to that plan . . . and made changes when need

Kevin Stefanski during a practice session on August 8, 2021
(ERIK DROST/WIKIMEDIA COMMONS)

be . . . was just incredible. Not only is he unflappable, he's also diverse. The 2020 Browns were going to do whatever they had to do to win. Maybe one game it was running the ball, maybe another game it was passing the ball. Let's just do whatever we have to do to win the game."

Preseason Super Bowl hopes were dashed when Stefanski's Browns slipped to 8-9 in his second season of 2021.

"I think the 2021 season was definitely a learning experience for Stefanski in calling plays," King said, "and that's the complaint that I have and a lot of other people have, that there were play calls that you kind of scratched your head about. I think the Browns needed to run the ball more, that was their personality. I think their offensive line was a much better run-blocking line than it was a pass-blocking line. Time and time again in 2021, we'd get stretches where they were running the ball and running the ball, and all of a sudden they're passing, and I'm wondering why. You always have to wonder when the head coach is calling offensive plays, 'Is it too much?' The head coach is the CEO, but can he also be the guy running out and doing some of the deliveries?"

OFFENSE

QUARTERBACK

THE CANDIDATES

Otto Graham
Frank Ryan
Brian Sipe
Bernie Kosar

Otto Graham is not a bad place to start when it comes to ranking the all-time best quarterbacks in Browns history. Ironically, Graham was not Cleveland's starting quarterback in the team's first-ever game at home against the Miami Seahawks on September 6, 1946. That distinction goes to a guy by the name of Cliff Lewis, who enjoyed a fine six-year career with the Browns as mainly a defensive back. Graham was the Tom Brady of that era. He led the Browns to 10 championship games, seven of which they won, from 1946 to 1955. He led the All-America Football Conference or NFL in at least one passing category in eight of his 10 seasons. He threw for at least 2,700 yards five times in an era when passing was secondary to running the ball. He threw at least 20 touchdown passes three times, including a career high of 25 in both 1947 and 1948. Graham was the AAFC United Press Most Valuable Player in 1948 and was the NFL UP MVP in 1953 and 1955. He was First-Team All-Pro from 1947 to 1949, in 1951, and from 1953 to 1955. He was

Otto Graham running for a first down against the Rams in the NFL championship game on Christmas Eve 1950 (*WORLD-TELEGRAM AND SUN*)

picked for the Pro Bowl from 1950 to 1955. He was enshrined in the Pro Football Hall of Fame in 1965.

A second-round draft pick out of Penn State University in 1957, Milt Plum became the Browns' starter in 1958. He directed the Browns to fine win-loss records through 1961 and also a playoff loss to the Giants in 1958. In fact, he was a Pro Bowler in 1960 and 1961. His 1960 season was his best as he threw for nearly 2,300 yards, 21 touchdowns, and just five interceptions and led the NFL with a 110.4 passer rating.

Frank Ryan, acquired in a trade with the Los Angeles Rams before the season, became the starter halfway through 1962. He was the man under center for the next five-plus years. He will always be remembered for throwing three touchdown passes to Gary Collins in leading Cleveland to a stunning 27–0 upset of the Baltimore Colts in the 1964 NFL championship game. However, Ryan accomplished much more than just that in his time with the Browns. He threw 25 touchdown passes in both 1963 and 1964 and had 29 scoring strikes in 1966, a season in which he nearly topped the 3,000-yard mark.

After Ryan was benched early in the 1968 season after a slow start by the Browns, filling his role was veteran Bill Nelsen, who had been traded to the team from the Steelers before the season. Nelsen led the Browns to nine victories in their next 10 games, including seven consecutive wins in which they scored at least 30 points and three straight triumphs in which they tallied at least 45 points. Nelsen directed the Browns to consecutive NFL title-game appearances in 1968 and 1969 and another playoff berth in 1971. He was a Pro Bowler in 1969.

Nelsen was the starter through the opening game of the 1972 season, which was his last. Mike Phipps, who the Browns drafted in the first round in 1970 after trading Paul Warfield to Miami in a controversial move, took his place and did not do much for the next four seasons. He suffered a separated shoulder during the opening game of the 1976 season and was replaced by 1972 13th-round draft pick Brian Sipe. Phipps was traded the following spring. Sipe did not have the size or arm that Phipps had, but he had one very important intangible—he was a leader. He inspired his teammates greatly. In that 1976 season, Sipe completed more than 57 percent of his passes, the highest completion percentage by a Cleveland quarterback since Ryan all the way back in 1962. He also became the first Browns' signal-caller to throw more touchdowns than interceptions—17 to 14—since Nelsen in 1969. The Browns improved to 9-5 in 1976, a six-game improvement from the previous season. Sipe was having a decent season in 1977 when he was lost for the year to a separated left shoulder. A 5-2 start disintegrated into a last-place finish.

When Sam Rutigliano replaced Forrest Gregg (Dick Modzelewski coached the final game of 1977) as head coach the next season, Sipe quickly became one of the best quarterbacks in the NFL. In 1980, his magic led the Kardiac Kids to an 11-5 record and the AFC Central Division crown. Several games that year came down to the final moments, the Browns winning many of them. That year, he was the Associated Press NFL Player of the Year and the AFC UPI MVP. He was First-Team All-Pro and a Pro Bowler. Like his teammates, Sipe suffered a heavy hangover the following season as the Browns tumbled to 5-11 and last place. Sipe was benched in favor of Paul McDonald six games into the 1982 season. Sipe won his job back in 1983 and had a fine season in leading the Browns to the brink of the playoffs. He left the Browns to play for Donald Trump's New Jersey Generals of the United States Football League.

After McDonald, who inherited the starting job, threw interception after interception in a disaster of a 1984 season, the Browns' fortunes changed dramatically when they selected former Miami (Fla.) standout quarterback—and Boardman, Ohio, native—Bernie Kosar in the 1985 NFL supplemental draft. With Kosar at the controls, Cleveland qualified for the playoffs five straight years from 1985 to 1989, including four division titles and three trips to the AFC Championship Game, all defeats to Denver. Kosar passed for almost 4,000 yards in 1986. He completed 33 of 64 passes for a team-record 489 yards in a dramatic 23–20 double-overtime divisional playoff win over the New York Jets on January 3, 1987. Kosar was a Pro Bowler the next season. Two-and-a-half seasons for Kosar under Bill Belichick was enough for Belichick—Kosar was unceremoniously released halfway through the 1993 season, ironically with the team tied for first place. The season went down the tubes after that.

After three seasons with no NFL football due to the original Browns relocating to Baltimore after the 1995 season, the city of Cleveland welcomed with open arms number one draft choice Tim Couch from the University of Kentucky in 1999 as the new, expansion Browns began play. Couch was pretty average during his five years leading the Browns. Admittedly, there wasn't much around him. He did lead the team to a playoff berth in 2002. Since then, all the way through 2017, the Browns went through quarterbacks like they were going out of style. Bad quarterbacks came and went, came and went. The topper was the 2017 season in which the Browns, with DeShone Kizer calling the signals, finished 0-16.

Number one draft pick Baker Mayfield, out of the University of Oklahoma, came aboard in 2018. Though not sensational, he quickly gave Browns fans reason for hope, showing glimpses of greatness. In 2020, he led the Browns to the postseason and a most satisfying playoff win at Pittsburgh. Mayfield's numbers had been mostly well above average, his best season coming in that 2020 campaign when he threw 26 touchdown passes

Baker Mayfield preparing to pass against Buffalo in a preseason game on August 17, 2018 (ERIK DROST/WIKIMEDIA COMMONS)

and only eight interceptions. Although he suffered through an injury-plagued 2021 season, many Browns fans believed he was the real deal and had them thinking that the team had finally found its long-awaited quarterback of the future. However, following the acquisition of Deshaun Watson, Mayfield was traded to the Carolina Panthers.

The four quarterbacks in the running for all-time best Browns quarterback are Graham, Ryan, Sipe, and Kosar.

OTTO GRAHAM

Where do you start with Otto Graham? One of the greatest quarterbacks in NFL history, Graham, in his 10-year career, never felt what it was like not to play in a championship game. Ten years, 10 championship games, seven of which he won.

"You ask Joe Montana who the greatest quarterback of all time is, and he'll tell you right up front, 'Otto Graham,'" said Steve King. "There was never more of a winner than Otto Graham. Everybody gets enamored now with, 'Oh, he threw for 400 yards and three touchdowns' and 'He was 21-out-of-25.' That's all good. That's great. But did you win the game? It's the quarterback's job to win the game. He's the only guy who touches the ball on every offensive play. The personality of every team is its quarterback. You think of the Patriots, you think of Tom Brady, you think of the Steelers with all those great defensive players, you think of Terry Bradshaw, you think of the 49ers, you think of Joe Montana. You have to have a great quarterback, and Graham was that. And he was at his best in the postseason. He was a tough guy, too."

If Graham was around today, they would be writing books about him and they would be making movies, too, and he'd be on the cover of every magazine. He was unbelievable. He was surrounded by great people, but he was the unquestioned leader. He was the guy, it was his huddle, everybody knew that. When the going got rough, he played his best. He took it upon himself to make sure the Browns won the game.

"Jim Brown is usually called the greatest player in Browns history, but I'd have to say that Otto Graham was the greatest player in team history," Bob Dolgan said. "When a running back has a great game, he runs for 150, 160, 170 yards. When a quarterback has a great game, he passes for 300, 400 yards. So just by the nature of the position, I think Graham was the greatest in team history."

"If you're going to make a Mount Rushmore of NFL quarterbacks, Graham very well might have to be included," said Ray Yannucci. "His record was unbelievable."

Graham could throw the bomb but also had great touch on his passes. Wrote Paul Brown, Graham's head coach for his entire professional career, in his autobiography *PB: The Paul Brown Story*, "I remember [Otto's] tremendous peripheral vision and his great skill, as well as his ability to throw a football far and accurately with just a flick of his arm."

"Otto Graham was one of the greatest throwers of all time," said Hall of Fame wide receiver Tom Fears, who played nine seasons for the Los Angeles Rams, in the NFL Films documentary *The NFL's Greatest Games—Volume II*.

When Brown removed Graham from the game toward the end of a 38–14 rout of the Rams in Los Angeles in the 1955 NFL title game, Graham's last game, the Coliseum crowd responded with a standing ovation, which dumbfounded Graham. "You don't find that happening too often in professional sports, where the opposition—the fans—who hate your guts, to put it mildly, will stand up and give you a standing ovation," he fondly recalled in the NFL Films documentary *The Cleveland Browns: Fifty Years of Memories*.

Summed up an emotional Brown in the same documentary, "When he [Graham] got to the sideline, he walked over to me and said, 'Thanks, Coach.' And I said, 'Thank you too, Otto.' That's all that was said."

FRANK RYAN

In his fourth year with the Browns, Frank Ryan earned a PhD in mathematics from Rice University. He understood the passing game as much as he understood mathematics.

"Frank was very smart. He was always thinking," said Ernie Green, mainly a Browns halfback from 1962 to 1968. "He was also tough and very good in difficult situations. He'd contribute any way he could, throwing the ball or running the ball. He had it all."

"I enjoyed playing with Frank immensely," Paul Warfield said. "I was a very young player just learning the passing game my rookie year, but he was a tremendous help to me and very instrumental to my initial success. He was perhaps the best long-ball thrower who I played with in my entire career. He had a great ability to throw the long post pattern, and he also had the ability to throw the take-off pattern down the field."

"Ryan was a big-armed guy who was one of the best deep passers I've seen," said Mike Peticca. "You always knew the Browns could strike from anywhere with him throwing to Collins or Warfield. He was also very good in the clutch. Those teams had very good pass-blocking with those great offensive lines, but he still took some hits, and he'd always get up. He didn't look great doing it, but he was really good at tucking the ball under and making runs to elude the pass rush. He made some big plays with his feet. He was fun to watch."

Said Gary Collins, a Browns wide receiver from 1962 to 1971, "I had a good relationship with Frank as far as communicating on and off the field. A lot of people felt Frank was weird, but he *was* weird. The guy is a genius. The man is brilliant, and you have to respect him for that. He had to work hard to 'come down' to be 'one of the guys.'"

"He was cerebral, just a tremendous player," Steve King said. "What a smart guy he was," Dan Coughlin added.

"You look at Ryan's stats from 1963-67," said King, "and in that five-year period they were better than anybody's in the league."

Although he continued to churn out solid statistics, what happened at the end of the 1964 season started Ryan on a slow downturn. With the Browns leading 27–0—including three touchdown passes to Collins—late in the NFL title game against Baltimore, Ryan tried to go deep once more. He wanted Warfield to get a touchdown. The Colts resented that, especially left defensive end Gino Marchetti. Marchetti got his revenge in the Pro Bowl two weeks later when he leveled Ryan in the shoulder.

"After that," said King, "Ryan was still very good but never quite the same."

"The '67 season might've been the start of Ryan's true decline," said Peticca. "I think he started losing a little bit of his mobility in certain games in which he just got punished."

Ryan was benched after three games in 1968 and was replaced by Bill Nelsen.

BRIAN SIPE

When Brian Sipe was drafted by the Browns, he didn't take it all that seriously. He figured he would stick around and have a good time until he was cut. When the Browns drafted quarterback Randy Mattingly the next year, that got Sipe's attention. He got serious about pro football.

"He would sit in the film room," said Jerry Sherk, who played right defensive tackle for the Browns from 1970 to 1981, in the summer 2004 edition of *Bernie's Insiders*, "and see things happen and think, 'Why didn't the quarterback do this?' or 'Gee, all he had to do was flip the ball to this guy.' He finally began to realize he could play ball."

"I noticed every time he got in there in an exhibition game, he was moving the ball and the team was moving down the field," Bob Dolgan said. "I said, 'Gee, this guy must have something, he's doing something right.'"

Sipe earned the backup quarterback spot behind starter Mike Phipps in 1974 after two years on the practice squad. He finally got his shot that season when he relieved a struggling Phipps late in a midseason home game against Denver. Sipe scored two late touchdowns to lead his team to a tight win. That earned him the starting job for the next five games, two of which the Browns won. He started two games in 1975.

"It was apparent early on that he was a special competitor," said Mike Peticca. "There were a variety of little passes and a couple short touchdown runs. Right away, he was somebody who people liked just because it was obvious that he wasn't big and didn't have a great arm but that he worked so hard to get the most out of his ability. He was obviously very smart."

However, on the day of the 1976 season opener, Sipe remained the backup behind Phipps. Phipps, though, got injured that day against the New York Jets, effectively ending his season. Sipe came in and put the finishing touches on a 38–17 Browns victory. He went on to have a fine season in leading the team to a 9-5 record. Phipps was traded the following spring. The next season, Sipe was having a pretty good year when he suffered a season-ending separated left shoulder during a crucial midseason defeat to the Steelers. The team tumbled from first place to last place by season's end.

"Brian was developing into a starting quarterback," said Paul Warfield. "He was a young guy with a lot of competitive fire. He certainly had the tools to play the position, and one could tell that his future was really developing. He certainly had command of the huddle. He understood what needed to be done. He commanded presence as a quarterback calling the plays, and one could tell that his leadership was evolving."

When Sam Rutigliano came aboard as head coach in 1978, Sipe knew once and for all that the starter's job was his. That season, the Browns trailed the Bengals, 10–0, at halftime in the second game of the year. "Things weren't going very well offensively," Rutigliano recalled. "About midway through the third quarter, Brian came up to me and said, 'Coach, I. . . .' I said, 'Look, don't even ask me. You're . . . my . . . quarterback. You're gonna be the quarterback. I want you to know that that's the decision that's already been made. I believe in you.' And then he got us in position to kick the winning field goal, and we won the game."

According to Rutigliano, connecting with people is key, but doing it at critical times like that is crucial. "You can encourage them and let them know, 'Hey, listen buddy, you don't have to worry,'" he said. "I could see the way Brian connected with his teammates. He gets the crap beat out of him, his helmet's almost turned around, and he goes back in the huddle and says, 'My fault, guys, my fault.' The players loved him. Brian empowered everyone around him, including special teams, including the defense, and certainly the offense, to play at a level they never dreamed they could play at."

"Sipe was as tough as they come, a winner," said Steve King. "The story, as Rutigliano tells it . . . when he was evaluating Sipe when he took over as head coach, he talked to Sipe's father, and Brian had been the catcher on a Little League World Series team. Even as a young kid, Brian Sipe was a winner. He just needed to believe in himself."

In 1979, Sipe was becoming one of the finest quarterbacks in the NFL. The Browns barely missed the playoffs. In

1980, he *was* the best quarterback in the league. He passed for 4,132 yards with 30 touchdowns and just 14 interceptions. The majority of games during both the 1979 and 1980 seasons came down to the wire, and the Browns, with Sipe leading the way, became known as the Kardiac Kids. Rutigliano compared Sipe to perhaps the greatest clutch player in another sport's history.

Brian Sipe (JERRY COLI/DREAMSTIME.COM)

"Michael Jordan. Sixth game. [1998] NBA Finals. The Bulls are down by one point [to Utah]. Less than 10 seconds to go," he said. "Four guys have grapefruits in their esophagus. Not Michael. He hit the game-winner. Brian had that same crave-the-moment 'it' factor about him. A lot of guys tell you that a quarterback is like a tea bag . . . you know . . . a lot of them get in hot water. But Brian craved the moment. He loved it, he absolutely loved it."

"Brian was just a great competitor," said Doug Dieken. "He was a guy who was smart and, what people don't realize about him, he was tough. He'd take a shot, he'd get back up. He had maybe five concussions in his time. He'd go in the huddle and call a play, and sometimes it wasn't a play we had. He was a great teammate. He was the league's Player of the Year in 1980, but he was always just one of the guys. He didn't have a big ego for the success that he had. He was a darned good quarterback, too."

In that 1980 season, whenever the Browns needed a pass made, Sipe made it. He was the leader of that team. He was the guy everybody looked up to. They blocked for him and performed for him. "I really think," King recalled, "it was the greatest single season a Browns quarterback has ever had in terms of making big plays and just being the guy time after time after time. Even when defenses were prepared to stop him, he still made plays."

"Sam was the architect, but Brian was the triggerman of the Kardiac Kids," said Ray Yannucci. "That, to me, was the most exciting era in Browns history, even including Paul Brown's era and the Marty Schottenheimer era. There was nothing to embrace like the Kardiac Kids. It was short term, only a couple years, but it was totally unbelievable what those teams did and how they were accepted. Those two years were like a magic carpet ride. Those teams are folklore quality."

"I thought Brian was tremendous," said Joe DeLamielleure. "He could see the field. If you gave him any time at all, he was impossible to sack. I swear, he had the best vision of any quarterback I've ever seen. He was one of those guys who looked downfield one way but he could see the whole field. He was just amazing, the throws he made. He was pretty good staying in the pocket."

"Brian was probably, pound for pound, as good of a player as there was," said Mike McLain. "I mean, you look at him, and he never should've been playing in the NFL. If you took Brian's heart for the game into Mike Phipps's body, you'd have one of the best quarterbacks ever. Sipe just overcame physical deficiencies to take the Browns to levels they never should've gotten to."

"Brian got as much out of his talent as he could," Peticca said.

"The players loved Brian, adored him because of his guts," said Dan Coughlin.

Said Reggie Rucker, a Browns wide receiver from 1975 to 1981, "He was a born leader."

BERNIE KOSAR

Not too many professional athletes wanted to play for a Cleveland team in the mid-1980s.

Bernie Kosar was the exception.

Because executive vice president / general manager Ernie Accorsi was able to manipulate his way to selecting Kosar with the first pick of the 1985 NFL supplemental draft, the Boardman native and lifelong Browns fan got his wish.

"Bernie came at the perfect time," said Steve King. "It was a storybook situation … a kid growing up in Boardman, he rooted for Brian Sipe, and in essence he followed Sipe as quarterback of the Browns. The Browns worked the supplemental draft to outsmart the Houston Oilers, and it just worked out. A high-profile athlete like that . . . it meant a lot to the Cleveland fans."

"I don't know if I can think of any player in Browns history whose arrival was more anticipated and valued than it was for Bernie," Ray Yannucci said. "I was at the press conference at the old stadium when they introduced him. I remember driving home and turning the radio on. All the stations were going crazy.

"The '70s were a dark decade, and then there were the Kardiac Kids, but that was just a two-year deal. So it had been a while since the team had had [sustained] success when Kosar arrived. The fans were hungry back then for a winner. To have a local boy announce to the world that he wanted to play for the Browns . . . you could not have scripted that any better as for the timing of it."

Kosar commanded respect from his Browns teammates right from the start. "Ozzie Newsome told me this story," said Mike McLain. "Bernie comes in as a rookie against New England [when Gary Danielson got injured during the game], and all the veterans in that huddle were chattering. Bernie went in that huddle, stood there for a minute, listened, and screamed at them, 'Shut up! This is my huddle. I'm running this team now.' Newsome later said, 'When he did that, they all looked at him and shut up. I was thinking, That kid is going to be something special because he had the nerve to tell a bunch of veteran players, before he threw a pass in the NFL, to shut up.' Kosar made some big plays in that game. New England was a tough team."

When Kosar took over for Danielson, the veteran quarterback knew Kosar had what it took to be a successful quarterback in the NFL. "Everything was there. Even his mental approach was there," he said in the September 2005 *Bernie's Insiders*. "There were some minor things that had to be done, cleaned up, wiped off and gotten ready to go. I knew he would do well. There's a language of understanding, a communication language between quarterbacks. I felt right off that Bernie understood the game. I knew he had different physical tools than maybe the layman saw, but I knew his understanding of the game and how he could communicate it with me made him a potential special player."

If you look at the great quarterbacks in history, for the most part, they all come in and right off the bat have success. "Look at Kosar's first regular-season game against New England," said King. "The Patriots went to the Super Bowl that year, and the Browns beat them. Bernie right away was successful. He took a team that had been 5-11 the year before and, all of a sudden, they go 8-8 and win the Central Division title. Now, a lot of that was due to [running backs] Earnest Byner and Kevin Mack, but a lot of it was having stability at quarterback with Kosar. And when he struggled his rookie year, as all rookies sometimes do, there was Gary Danielson.

"By '86, those struggling times were behind Kosar. He was set to go. You saw a lot of that in '85, but he couldn't really show what he was made of because the offense was not a sophisticated offense. You saw that in the playoff game at Miami, and he got mad about it and demanded a change."

"After the Browns got that 21–3 lead in the playoff game at Miami," Mike Peticca recalled, "I think it's obvious that anyone would see that the limitations of their offense being so simple at that time cost them the game probably. So not only did they really slow down after the 21–3 lead, but it was pretty evident the lack of sophistication, the lack of diversity, in the offense, that they really didn't have many go-to pass plays in the playbook. It all just made them easier to defend as far as the simplicity of what they were showing to defenses. And it was especially evident after Miami took the 24–21 lead in the fourth quarter. You could see that they didn't have much of a way to really attack unless they were going to maybe break a big play like Byner's earlier long run. They just didn't pose enough problems for a defense. And I think in the aftermath of that, Marty Schottenheimer realized he had to branch out further in how he looked at how games should be prepared for tactically and then executed. I think Bernie made Marty become a better coach, a better all-around coach, with his fingers on every aspect of the game."

Bernie Kosar (JERRY COLI/DREAMSTIME.COM)

Lindy Infante was brought in the next season as the Browns' offensive coordinator and—voila!—a great passing offense was born. The team made two straight trips to the AFC Championship Game in 1986 and 1987. "Those two seasons were fantastic years of growth at quarterback for the Browns, Infante, Danielson, and Kosar," said King. "It was a lot of cerebral guys in there, and Bernie picked up on that, kept his eyes open, and listened to what those guys had to say. It was a great quarterback situation. Bernie sponged off of those guys, took everything they said, and combined that with his own intellect. He was really in tune those two years. With Bernie, you had another coach on the field."

The Browns' offense was so much more advanced and sophisticated in 1986 and 1987. It was much more diverse. It allowed the Browns to take greater advantage of the very good offensive talent they had at the skill positions and behind a very good line.

Mike Baab will never forget the first time he saw Kosar.

"I remember looking at him and saying, 'That's the tallest 12-year-old I've ever seen,' he recalled in the September 2005 *Bernie's Insiders*. "When he first got here, he wasn't much in the way of physique."

"Kosar was a quarterback who really performed better than his physical attributes would allow," Yannucci said. "An 80-year-old grandmother could've looked at the TV and seen that he didn't run that well. But he could see things before they happened, and when a quarterback can do that, sometimes you can overcome physical limitations. Kosar was a tremendous overachiever based on his physical qualities . . . slow, awkward, sidearm but a brilliant football mind. He came pretty close to winning Super Bowls. If it wasn't for this play or that play . . . he was a winner."

"He was a great quarterback," said King. "He wasn't the prettiest thing, but you know what? He got the job done. And he, to me, was rising to become one of the best quarterbacks in the league. There was no question about it. He did the one thing right from the start that a lot of quarterbacks, even in their later years, don't do. He'd look one way and throw the other way. Quarterbacks lock in on receivers and they throw to them, and they wonder why the ball gets batted down or picked off. It never gets completed because they eyed the receiver the whole way. But Bernie was as good as anybody at looking the other way. He looked off the defenders and made sure they didn't know where the pass was going. For all of his maybe physical deficiencies, the mobility and this, that, and the other, his ability to read defenses and to find the weak spots in them and to spread the ball around ... that's a fantastic trait to have for any quarterback, and he had it, and I think that was his biggest strength."

Kosar had great anticipation and accuracy. The receiver had not even begun to come out of his break, and the ball was already in the air. He had tremendous timing with that part of it. Combine his intelligence with his anticipation and the subsequent accuracy—those were the things that enabled him to be so efficient.

"They [his teammates] recognized he had the ability to do it and the leadership to enable us to function efficiently as an offense," Schottenheimer said in the September 2005 *Bernie's Insiders*. "It became obvious he was the leader of the offensive football team, if not the [entire] football team. It just makes it a little bit easier when the guy has the intellectual capability that Bernie had. You can give him more information that can be processed and learned and ultimately applied more quickly when it's done that way. He had some of those (Joe) Montana qualities because of his anticipation and confidence in what he was doing. I don't think Bernie ever thought a game was out of reach regardless of the circumstances because he had so much confidence in himself. He was a guy who found ways to win football games. He may not have been the prototype in terms of what you're looking at—big, physical, strong-armed, great athletic skills. He didn't necessarily have those qualities, but that didn't matter. He found a way to make it work."

"Bernie played in an era when there were nine future Pro Football Hall of Fame quarterbacks," Yannucci said. "While he did not have the credentials of those Hall of Famers, he certainly was an exceptional team leader in the mold of Tom Brady. Also, what he lacked in athletic ability, he made up for it with his cerebral approach to the position. He was a winner. I used to refer to him as the iconic number 19."

"He was probably the smartest quarterback the Browns have had since Frank Ryan," said Jeff Schudel. "That's what really set him apart from everybody who followed him. That's what made Bernie what he was. And he did have a good arm and had a great rapport with his receivers . . . Webster Slaughter and Reggie Langhorne and Brian Brennan and Ozzie Newsome. He had a connection with those guys. Bernie's offensive line really took pride in protecting him knowing that he wasn't the most mobile guy around."

After the 1987 season, Infante left to become head coach of the Green Bay Packers. Nonetheless, the Browns were perhaps the popular choice in the AFC to get to the Super Bowl in 1988. "I think there was a sense that that '88 team was going to be maybe the best of the teams of that era to that point," Peticca said. "Of course, Bernie hurt his elbow in the opening game at Kansas City. Not only did it hamper Bernie to some extent then and of course caused him to miss numerous games, but I don't think he was quite the same throwing the ball after that. If he hadn't fallen prey to the injuries he did beginning in '88, I think he would've had a much longer career possibly and with several more prime seasons ahead even though he continued to be rather effective and sometimes brilliant over the next several years. There's no doubt the injuries limited him showing his maximum abilities over a long period of time. And who knows how far the Browns would've gone in '88? Obviously, Danielson, Mike Pagel, and Don Strock had some heroic efforts, but it wasn't the same as having a healthy Bernie in there."

"You saw what happened in the first game Infante was gone, somebody misses a pickup on a blitz, Bernie gets hit, and that's history," said King. "The offense in '88 didn't look as crisp and explosive as it had in '86 and '87. I think, had Infante stayed in '88 and Bernie not gotten hurt—which I think would've happened because you wouldn't have seen that kind of dysfunction in Kansas City—I think there would've been a whole different story written. There's no question in my mind that, had Bernie not gotten hurt in the opening game of 1988, he would've taken the Browns to not just the Super Bowl, but he would've taken them to several Super Bowls, and I think they would've won one or two of them. There's no question in my mind, that team was primed for that, but it just didn't work out."

"It's a shame," said Accorsi in the September 2005 *Bernie's Insiders*. "History will never treat (Kosar's legacy) to its merit because we didn't win the Super Bowl. To go to three championship games in four years and the playoffs five straight seasons was a remarkable run. There were certain things that happened that we just were unlucky. In my opinion, we were unequivocally the best team in the AFC and maybe in football when the strike hit in 1987. We had just absolutely blown the Steelers out. We were at the top of our game coming off the confidence of 1986. We were healthy. We were powerful. The strike broke our momentum. We never got back to that dominance. The problem in today's society is if you don't win a world championship, then the era's not great. It sure was a great run. We came so close.

"The thing about (Kosar) was he was a unique figure. He didn't necessarily look like an athlete. Someone once told me he looked like the conductor of a philharmonic orchestra with all that hair. He was tall, lanky. He was underrated in certain aspects of his athleticism. He certainly couldn't run, but he had quick feet and he had a quick release. He was brilliant. From the time he saw something and got rid of the ball, it negated his lack of mobility . . . he had a magic about him. It's a shame he didn't win a championship. He had a Hall of Fame five years (1985–89)."

"All you have to look at when talking about Bernie is the fact that the Browns played in three AFC Championship Games in four years with him there," Schudel said. "They didn't do that before him and haven't done it since."

Kosar will go down as one of the most beloved players in Browns history. He is certainly an icon in the eyes of Browns fans.

Said Jim Brown, "Very unselfish and loved tremendously by the Cleveland Brown fans."

"He's still, to this day," Yannucci said, "one of the most popular Browns players, if not the most popular Browns player, ever."

And the Winner Is . . .

Paul Brown brought a passing game first to the AAFC and then to the NFL that neither had ever seen before. And that passing game was fueled by none other than Otto Graham. Graham led the AAFC and NFL in so many passing categories and won so many awards, it would make your head spin. The most important thing he won, however, was championships, and his Browns teams won seven. Coincidentally, that is the same number of titles Tom Brady has won. But it took Brady 21 seasons to accomplish the feat. Graham did it in 10 years.

Frank Ryan is largely responsible for the Browns' last NFL championship. Yes, he had a magnificent game in the team's 27–0 shocker over the Colts in the 1964 title contest, but Ryan was far from a one-hit wonder. He had some very solid seasons for the Browns from 1963 to 1967, leading the league in touchdown passes in 1964 and 1966. Was he Otto Graham? No, but who was? Ryan had a very good career with the Browns.

The ultimate overachiever was Brian Sipe. With his small stature and not-exactly-strong arm, he was not expected to make the team, let alone win the NFL Player of the Year honor, when he was drafted by the Browns. To make up for his deficiencies, he was smart, he was accurate—even on the long throws—and he was a heck of a leader. He got more out of his abilities than maybe any other player in NFL history.

It should come as no surprise that Bernie Kosar graduated from college in three years. He was that smart. And he proved it on the football field right from his very first action in an NFL game his rookie year. He could read defenses like few quarterbacks in the history of the league ever have. He had touch on his passes, even when he threw the bomb. He led the Browns to three AFC title games in four years, taking Browns fans on a wild ride they will never forget.

It really was not a tough decision at all to pick **Otto Graham** as the Browns' all-time best quarterback.

QUARTERBACKS WHO DID NOT MAKE THE CUT

Milt Plum piled up some very good statistics in his last two seasons with the Browns. Even he admitted, however, that those stats may have been a tad deceiving.

"Some games, things go well for you," he said. "Somebody makes a great catch . . . of course, that benefits you. You throw a

10-yard sideline pass and—boom!—the guy runs 80 yards with it and you get credit for a 90-yard touchdown pass. And a lot of my passes were just that—screens where we dumped the ball off to Jim Brown and Bobby Mitchell and let them run. But then some games, you hit the receiver right in the chest, the ball bounces up, it's intercepted, and it goes against you."

Plum believes he gets a bad rap when people say he couldn't throw the bomb. "We almost never called for the long ball," he said. "These days, you think of [Tom] Brady and guys like that . . . you know . . . they're passers. We just didn't throw the ball nearly as much as these guys today. We played Pittsburgh once and I threw 10 passes. That's unheard of in this day and age. They throw it 10 times in one quarter now!"

"Plum was a very good quarterback," said Steve King. "He was one of those guys who Paul Brown looked at in trying to find his next Otto Graham. And he never really did. Plum was more of a system quarterback. He wasn't a long thrower. He was a short passer, an accurate passer. He wasn't the leader that Graham had been. He was the kind of quarterback who Brown liked in that when you told him to do something, he did it very well. He was a very accurate passer."

"He was a good mechanical quarterback," said Bob Dolgan.

Bill Nelsen was given a reprieve. After toiling for five seasons with a Pittsburgh Steelers team going nowhere as usual, the scrappy quarterback was traded to the Browns, one of the NFL's elite teams, in the spring of 1968.

"It was quite a thrill to go and play with a championship caliber team like the Browns. The offensive line I had in Pittsburgh wasn't even close to the great line I came to in Cleveland," said Nelsen, who, even while dealing with knee issues, helped keep the Browns one of the best teams in the NFL.

The Browns put Nelsen in and the offense just purred right from the get-go. He was a great leader and as tough a quarterback as the Browns have ever had, maybe a little tougher even. His knees were worse than Joe Namath's. "He was a very, very good quarterback during the 1968 and '69 seasons," King said. "He made plays when he had to. He was very strong in the short to intermediate passing routes. He was a very, very accurate thrower."

"Nelsen was a great quarterback, but he had those bad knees," said Bob Dolgan. "He was a winner, no doubt about it. He could inspire a team the way Sipe and Kosar could."

Nelsen was a tremendous competitor. He was not very tall, so he had to know exactly where the receivers were on every play because he could not always see them. He knew who was doing the job on their guy on the line. He knew where to run the ball when the team needed to run it.

"Bill's teammates really respected him and admired him. He had guts," Dan Coughlin said.

"I think he was what you could call an above-average quarterback," said Ray Yannucci. "His problem was bad knees, and that was the reason why Art Modell traded Paul Warfield to the Dolphins to get the rights to draft Mike Phipps, which was probably one of the four or five major gaffes of Modell's tenure in Cleveland."

Despite the arrival of Deshaun Watson, the Cleveland fan base was split down the middle as to whether **Baker Mayfield** was the Browns' quarterback of the future. King was on the positive side and actually believed Mayfield was even better than the positive people thought.

"There's a reason for that," he said. "I watch Ohio State football a lot, and there are two people who I've seen come into Columbus, and even with all those five-star defensive backs and all those great defensive players, put the ball in places that even those guys couldn't have been and beat Ohio State with their arm. One was a guy by the name of John Elway, who did it with

Stanford in 1982. The other was Baker Mayfield, who did it in 2017 with Oklahoma. You couldn't have laid the ball in there any better if you ran out and handed it to those Sooners receivers. Time after time after time, when Mayfield needed to make a play, he made it. It was incredible. Ohio State didn't play bad defense, he just played great offense.

"When the Browns drafted Mayfield, I knew the thing that had bothered a lot of the Browns' quarterbacks before—accuracy—was not going to be a problem with this guy. He did have some accuracy problems in some spots the first year or two, but he's a guy who's a winner, he's an accurate passer, he understands the game, he's a gym rat for a quarterback. He played well in a very high-powered college conference at a school that's traditionally great, he played under a great offensive mind in Lincoln Riley there. He has all the prerequisites. The only thing he doesn't have is height. Well, say what you want about Brian Sipe. He wasn't very big either, but he was able to find lanes to throw the ball through and was able to find ways to get the ball where it needed to go. Mayfield is a guy who will do that as well.

"None of the turnaround with the Browns happens without Baker Mayfield. You can have Nick Chubb and you can have Kareem Hunt and you can have Myles Garrett and this player and that player, but it starts with the quarterback. And, to me, Mayfield was by far the best quarterback the Browns have had since Bernie Kosar. Was he a franchise quarterback? Yes, without question because you could build a team around him and, as the games got tougher and more important, he made more plays. The playoff game against Kansas City in 2020, he puts the ball right in the receiver's hands. The receiver drops it at the two-yard line. That's not Mayfield's fault. That game was ripe for an upset."

An early-season left shoulder injury in 2021 was no doubt the reason for Mayfield's failures that season, according to King. "They talk about the injury being to the non-throwing shoulder," he said, "but opening up that shoulder is part of the throwing motion, and when that isn't right, your throw is not going to be right. If you go back and look at some of Mayfield's throws he made after the injury as opposed to before the injury and certainly all of the season before, you'd see a drastic difference. In baseball, guys have to change their motion a little bit when injured, and it's the same thing in football. All of a sudden, you miss a couple throws and you can't make the throws that you want, you start losing confidence, and you start to force the ball. The ball goes high. For Mayfield in 2021, his throws were high a lot of the time, off target. You're just not throwing comfortably. Your confidence isn't what it should be because you're not hitting those throws, things kind of pile up on each other and exacerbate each other, and all of a sudden you have a guy who didn't play as well as he did before. And I think that traces back to the injury. On top of that, Mayfield has never had a deep-threat wide receiver who can run down the field and make plays."

King was confident that Mayfield, if healthy, had the talent to lead the Browns to the promised land.

"If I was certain," he said, "that Mayfield was going to be with the Browns for an extended period of time, I say they not only go to a Super Bowl but win it because of him, because you have to have that guy. In today's game more than ever, you have to have a quarterback who can make plays in the fourth quarter. And Baker Mayfield was that quarterback, there's no question in my mind."

Jeff Schudel was not quite as high on Mayfield as King was, but he still believed he was a very good quarterback. "People remember that bad year in 2019," he said, "but I think you have to look back at 2018 and 2020 to draw the conclusion that 2019 was really an off year and he had everything going against him. The coaching staff was discombobulated and Ryan Lindley, the quarterbacks coach, wasn't ready for that job. When you talk about Baker Mayfield, you have to also include Kevin Stefanski because they really worked well together in 2020. Stefanski knew how to use Mayfield in a better way than Freddie Kitchens [the Browns' head coach in 2019] did. When Mayfield rolled out and found his receiver, he was accurate. He was also a good leader. The players responded to him."

Schudel's feelings about Mayfield were somewhat tempered by his 2021 season. "After four years," he said, "I think it's fair to say the Browns don't know exactly what they had in Baker Mayfield. And if you don't know after four years, it probably means that you don't have the right guy. The Browns were in a real pickle because they didn't know if Mayfield was the 2018 and '20 Mayfield or the 2019 and '21 Mayfield. Before you got rid of Mayfield and moved on, you had to have somebody better, and that would be difficult, I think, finding a better quarterback than Mayfield, which doesn't mean that he's anything special. But you couldn't just say, 'Okay, we have to get rid of Baker Mayfield,' and then what do you do? I think he's better than he showed in 2021, but he was too inconsistent. If everything was ideal, Mayfield was going to be good for you, but was he a quarterback who could step up when things were not ideal? Take the Chargers-Raiders 2021 regular-season finale. Justin Herbert of the Chargers was amazing. His team was down, it's fourth-and-21 or something like that, and he throws a touchdown pass! Baker Mayfield doesn't have that, I don't think he does. Herbert was only in his second season, and he's so much more decisive with the ball than Baker Mayfield."

FULLBACK

THE CANDIDATES

Marion Motley
Jim Brown
Nick Chubb

Marion Motley averaged—yes, averaged!—8.2 yards per rushing attempt in 1946. He gained 601 yards on just 73 carries. What more needs to be said? The 6-foot-1, 232-pound giant literally scared defenders, especially much smaller defensive backs, when he was running toward them. He looked like an approaching tank. He led the Browns in rushing yards six times. In 1948, he ran the ball 157 times for 964 yards with five touchdowns. He was First-Team All-Pro in 1948 and 1950 and a Pro Bowler in 1950. He was inducted into the Pro Football Hall of Fame in 1968.

The Browns hit the jackpot in 1957 by selecting Jim Brown in the first round of the NFL Draft out of Syracuse University. Brown's best season was 1963 when he rushed for 1,863 yards on 291 carries with 12 touchdowns. He had six other seasons in which he eclipsed 1,200 rushing yards. He had five seasons in which he rushed for at least a dozen touchdowns, including 17 in both 1958 and 1965. He averaged an astounding 104.3 yards rushing per game in his career, still an NFL record. He could also catch the ball. In 1961, he had 46 receptions for 459 yards with two touchdowns, and in 1962 he caught 47 passes for 517 yards with five touchdowns. Brown led the NFL in rushing yards in each of his nine seasons. He was the AP NFL Player of the Year in 1957 and 1965. He was the UPI NFL MVP in 1958, 1963, and 1965. He was First-Team All-Pro in all but one season—1962—and was a Pro Bowler every year. He was inducted into the Pro Football Hall of Fame in 1971.

Drafted in 1976 out of Purdue University, Mike Pruitt did not become one of the league's best fullbacks until 1979. The season before, first-year head coach Sam Rutigliano gave him his first real shot, and he produced. He rushed for at least 1,000 yards from 1979 to 1981 and in 1983. He very possibly could have had five straight seasons with 1,000 yards rushing if not for the 1982 players' strike. Pruitt's hands were not exactly the best in his first few seasons in the league, but he eventually became a prime target of Brian Sipe's. He caught 63 passes in both 1980 and 1981. He was a Pro Bowler in 1979 and 1980.

In Kevin Mack's rookie season of 1985, he rushed for 1,104 yards. He and halfback Earnest Byner became only the third running-back tandem in NFL history to each rush for 1,000 yards in one season. Mack had seven rushing touchdowns that year. In 1986, he ran for 10 touchdowns. He could also catch passes out of the backfield as he had 42 and 40 receptions, respectively, in 1990 and 1991. He was a Pro Bowler in 1985 and 1987.

There really wasn't much to speak of when it came to fullbacks after Mack until Nick Chubb was drafted in the second round out of the University of Georgia in 2018. Chubb has only been in the NFL for three years, but he has produced some remarkable numbers. As a rookie in 2018, he barely missed rushing for 1,000 yards and ran for eight touchdowns. The next season, he rushed the ball 298 times for 1,494 yards

Nick Chubb running with the football against the Steelers on November 14, 2019 (ERIK DROST/WIKIMEDIA COMMONS)

with eight touchdowns. In 2020, he missed four games but still totaled 1,067 rushing yards on 190 carries with 12 touchdowns. The next season, he had 228 rushes for 1,259 yards with eight touchdowns. Chubb's best receiving year was 2019 when he had 36 catches for 278 yards. He was a Pro Bowler from 2019 to 2021.

The three players who are in the running for greatest Browns fullback of all time are Motley, Brown, and Chubb.

MARION MOTLEY

Marion Motley was probably ahead of his time.

"Motley was a big, fast, powerful running back," said Ray Yannucci. "I think he could've played in any era."

"He was a classic fullback," said Bob Dolgan. "He weighed about 235 pounds when linemen were about 210 or 220. I remember a game in Municipal Stadium when he broke into the clear, and a cornerback had a chance to tackle him. Motley probably weighed 60 pounds more than him. And you could see the cornerback visibly frightened with Motley coming after him. Motley ran right over him. I remember a game in which he made one of the greatest runs anybody ever saw. He broke down the sideline. He got hit at least five times by different players. He went all the way in and staggered into the end zone for a touchdown. For a solid week, they were showing that play on television. It was just unbelievable. Motley wasn't just a big, strong guy, he was also very fast. Paul Zimmerman of *Sports Illustrated* called him the greatest player in the history of professional football. He also played linebacker in goal-line situations."

Motley did not receive the credit for how fast he was and how much of a great athlete he was. He was an unbelievably powerful guy, but he was also a good athlete. "The trap play was just perfect for him," Steve King said. "Here's a defensive tackle wondering why nobody is blocking him, and here comes a 240-pound fullback to run you over. You see some of those films, and he's literally running over top of people. It's unbelievable. We talk about Otto Graham, the receivers, and all that, but you had to be able to run the football. Motley was the perfect guy for that team."

JIM BROWN

Jim Brown may not only be the greatest *running back* in NFL history, he just might be the greatest *player* in league annals.

"Jimmy Brown, to me, was the best runner that I ever played against," said Ray Nitschke, an outstanding linebacker for the Green Bay Packers from 1958 to 1972, in an NFL Films documentary on Brown. "He had it all. He had great size, he had power, he had speed. But I think his biggest asset was that he was smart. He knew exactly where the defense was, he knew where his offensive players were, and he utilized all the talents that he had. He was just unreal."

"Brown was a very naturally gifted athlete," said Tom Melody, a longtime sportswriter and sports columnist for the *Akron Beacon Journal.* "When he ran with the ball, he looked like he was gliding. He never let his feet get too far off the ground."

"As a fan, you always felt that the Browns had a chance no matter who they were playing because of Brown," Mike Peticca said. "You always expected the spectacular runs. I always liked to see them use him as a receiver, too, throwing passes to him out in the flat, and once in a while they'd have him run downfield routes. He was very dangerous in that regard, too. You were always aware of his reputation of not being especially anxious to block, but you were willing to put up with that because he had to be the greatest runner of all time."

Brown was a physical freak. He was bigger than a lot of the linebackers and even some of the defensive ends! Combine that with his speed, and he was one of the most intimidating players ever. "I know Jim very well," said Ray Yannucci, "and obviously he's a very well-spoken, intelligent person but still very intimidating as far as his physical presence."

Don Meredith, the Cowboys' quarterback during the November 21, 1965, Browns game at Dallas, was so enthralled with a short touchdown run Brown made, he found himself actually applauding his opponent from the sideline.

"It was the greatest run I ever saw," he said in the NFL Films documentary *75 Seasons.* "He went left, and he came back right, and he came back left, and our guys kept hitting him, and they kept falling off. He bounced back and scored. And I'm on the sideline, and I just have never seen anything like this and I'm saying, 'Wow! God!' And then I realized that I was on the wrong side of this deal."

"Jimmy Brown did things humanly impossible," said Frank Gifford, who played 11 seasons for the New York Giants in the 1950s and '60s, in the documentary on Brown. "And I watched him do it over and over and over. You watch a film of Jimmy Brown running the football, and he's moving away from things that there's no way that he could see. They're instincts that other football players have never even thought of, I'm sure. He had all of that, plus he had the great determination to be the very best."

"Jimmy Brown obviously took more shots than any of these running backs today because he carried the ball more," said Steve Stonebreaker, mainly a linebacker for a handful of teams in the 1960s, in the documentary on Brown. "Everybody wanted to knock him down. He never wore hip pads, he never wore thigh pads. He only wore shoulder pads and a helmet, and everybody took their shots at Jimmy. He asked no quarters, he gave no quarters. He got up after every play."

Recalled Chuck Bednarik, a notoriously tough linebacker for the Philadelphia Eagles from 1949 to 1962, in *75 Seasons*, "You gang-tackled him, gave him extracurriculars. He'd get up slow, look at you, and walk back to that huddle and wouldn't say a word . . . just come at you again, and again. You'd just say, 'What the hell, what's wrong with this guy? For heaven's sake, when is he going to stop carrying the ball? How much more can he take?'"

This is where Brown's acumen came in.

"There are many ideas when you basically use your mind, your intelligence," Brown said. "The thing you try to do in any competition is get all of your advantages that you can get. And you never want to give your opponent any psychological advantage or any physical advantage. So, consequently, if you get up fast on 10 plays and then get up slow on the 11th, they know you're hurt. If you're hurt, they're going to be empowered. They're going to come at you twice as hard. You're motivating them to come and try to get you out of the game because you're showing the fact that they have been able to hurt you. So you try to be very consistent in your mannerism as you play a game because, that way, you don't encourage your opponents."

"He didn't even want his teammates and coaches to know he was hurting," said Melody. "If he went into the trainer's room after a game—and he didn't do it very often—he did not want anybody to see that he was in there."

"I tell people, 'I had a total knee replacement. That's because of Jim Brown. I have two bad shoulders. That's Jim Brown. I had two back operations. That's from Jim Brown.' I call them my 'Jim Browns,'" Dick Modzelewski laughed. Modzelewski, who played left defensive tackle, was Brown's teammate in 1964 and 1965, but he played *against* the great fullback for several years prior to that as a member of the New York Giants.

"It was better to play *with* Jim Brown than against him," continued Modzelewski. "To this day, they can tell me all they want about all these backs they have now . . . nobody compares to him. We were watching some game films one time, and Jim Brown is running the ball, and all you see are Giants, eight or nine of them, on top of this one person [Brown], moving. All of us were on him, grabbing him by the ankles, by the knees, anything we could possibly do."

Brown missed only one half of one game during his entire career. "I actually missed only a few plays," he said. "The bottom line is, after you get in condition, after you know what you're doing, after you have certain experiences, you have to be lucky because you can get hurt walking down the field. Individuals have gotten hurt just jogging. So luck plays a great part of it, but in order to make sure that you leave it only to luck, you have to be in great shape and you have to understand things that you do and don't do. And you play the game hard, but you don't do certain things that are basically going to lead to injuries. Every time you go up in the air, there's a chance that you can really get hurt. If you plant your foot and get hit on that particular leg, it's a chance that you can get hurt as you come back the wrong way. So you try to know how to maximize yourself without jeopardizing yourself.

"About 95 percent of everything I'm talking about comes from the mind. Basically, I was very proud of my body. I didn't want to be fat, I didn't want to be out of shape, I didn't want to be out of shape at *any* time of the year. I reported to camp about five pounds under weight, in good shape, and the coach would notice that right away, and then I was left alone. I played basketball, did different things, in the offseason. I made sure I stayed in great shape. I wanted my clothes to fit and I wanted to look as a fit individual. So it was just really being conscientious of my physical conditioning and having a way of keeping myself in shape. I didn't depend upon any coaches to motivate me to be in shape, I was self-motivated. Some of it was vanity, and the other was that I knew that if I was always in top shape, fatigue would never be a factor. Fatigue makes a coward out of all of us."

"Even though Jim played when there were 12- and 14-game seasons," said Paul Warfield, "had he played three more years, I'd go as far as to say that he'd own all of the rushing records in pro football."

"You were thinking he had a few more prime seasons," Peticca said. "It was just disappointing that Jim Brown wasn't going to be there anymore [when he retired in the summer of 1966]. I remember thinking, 'Well, there goes the safety blanket. They should still be pretty good, though, because of [Frank] Ryan, [Gary] Collins, and Warfield. Ernie Green is going to have to be the guy.'"

"Jim Brown," said Dick Schafrath, who played left offensive tackle for the Browns from 1959 to 1971, "was the actual

Jim Brown (MALCOLM W. EMMONS/THE SPORTING NEWS ARCHIVES)

tilting force in that group because we had some great players before and after him, but he just made that little difference. If he'd have stuck around, I think we might've gotten that Super Bowl."

Brown felt privileged to have played in Cleveland.

"We had 80,000 people, they loved our performances, I loved the fact that they *did* love my performances," he said. "They've been very forgiving of me over the years, they allowed me to step out of line once in a while. I was able even to speak nicely about Art Modell and they didn't crucify me. So I've always had, I think, a relationship with the Cleveland Browns' fans, and always will, because we shared history together. Those families grew up with me. I didn't grow up with them, but I was very cognizant with how they felt. And later on when I did my book [*Out of Bounds*], I realized that fathers and sons, and mothers and daughters, have been in those stands—season tickets—and when I performed on a high level, they were proud and happy about being together and having a shared experience."

Said Stonebreaker in the documentary on Brown, "I personally don't like Jimmy Brown . . . but I certainly had to respect him as a football player. To play nine years and only miss one half of one game with a broken wrist is remarkable."

Bobby Mitchell in *75 Seasons*: "Until you lined up next to this guy and watched him time after time make it come out alright for the Cleveland Browns, you can't fully respect how good he was. If we had the capabilities today to show him from 15 different angles, people would have said that was not a human."

Nick Chubb

Nick Chubb has not only taken the Browns by storm, he has taken the entire NFL by storm in his first four seasons in the league. He is such an electrifying runner. He is powerful and he breaks tackles. He is so fast after he gets a couple of steps, he just outruns opposing defenders. "He breaks long runs," said Jeff Schudel. "You watch him after he scores a touchdown, he doesn't pound his chest, he doesn't do anything to draw attention to himself. You want a humble guy, that's him."

"I think Nick epitomizes what you want in a football player. He just wants to win," said Doug Dieken. "His first season, he had a thousand yards rushing but got hit for a loss late in the last game and didn't get his thousand, but that didn't matter to him. He just wanted to win the football game. It's not about the stats with him, it's just about doing the best you can and trying to get wins."

"I like Nick Chubb a lot. How could you not? He keeps his mouth shut and plays," Steve King said. "He carried the Browns a lot in 2020. His speed, power, durability, breakaway speed, quickness . . . he's got it all. He's just a great player. You see a lot of the tradition of the Browns' great backs in Chubb. He's every bit the equal of some of those guys."

"Nick Chubb could play on my football team any day. I wish I had 11 of him," said Mike McLain. "I love every aspect about him. He hands the ball to the referee after he scores a la Barry Sanders. You win Super Bowls if you go out on the field with Nick Chubb."

AND THE WINNER IS . . .

Marion Motley ran with the football like he was a man among children. Defenders were not too keen on trying to tackle him. He was a load, that's for sure. He averaged an incredible 5.7 yards per rushing attempt in his career. To put that in perspective, consider that Jim Brown averaged 5.2 yards per rushing attempt in his career.

There were only two seasons in which Brown failed to rush for 1,000 yards, and both times he was close. Brown was as hard to tackle as just about any running back in pro football history. His 1,863 yards on the ground in 1963 were the NFL record until O. J. Simpson broke the mark a decade later. Brown retired while he was at his peak. Imagine what kind of numbers he would have piled up had he played four or five more years.

Nick Chubb has only played four seasons, but his numbers and his running ability make it pretty tough not to consider him for the honor of greatest Browns fullback ever. However, it is even tougher not to give that honor to **Jim Brown**, who gets our vote.

FULLBACKS WHO DID NOT MAKE THE CUT

When **Mike Pruitt** first came to Cleveland, he didn't really know what to expect.

"Being a first-round draft choice, I thought I was going to play early on, but that didn't happen," he said. "I had a few problems holding on to the ball, so I had to work on that. When I got benched, that was a blow to my ego. That's one of the things I learned from that era that helps me today. I don't care how good you are, you keep yourself up all the time. I learned that you're only as good as your teammates. That helped me long-term in the league, learning to play within my ability and also to play as a teammate, not as an individual."

Pruitt was in awe the first time he ran on to the Municipal Stadium field in the 1976 season opener. "I was thinking, 'I can't believe I'm actually here, competing with guys who I've watched for years!'" he remembered. "And the Cleveland fans were remarkable. I'd never seen anything like it."

"When Pruitt first came here, Forrest Gregg was the head coach, and I don't think Forrest really liked him," said Ray Yannucci. "He was a big, fast, powerful runner, but he had short arms, so he had a hard time catching passes. I don't think he endeared himself to Forrest because of that. When Sam Rutigliano came in in '78, he saw how good Pruitt could be, and that was the start of him having an exceptional career."

A 71-yard touchdown run he made against Buffalo on October 29, 1978, was the confidence boost Pruitt so desperately needed.

"For the first time, I truly believed I belonged in the NFL," he said.

"Pruitt struggled early on, had some fumbling problems, but occasionally his talent was evident even then," said Mike Peticca. "He's got to be regarded as one of the Browns' best pure running backs ever. He was just a great blend of power and speed. He worked hard to become maybe an adequate receiver because early on he had a lot of trouble catching the ball. But, just looking at the numbers, you can see that he made a lot of catches during the Kardiac Kids years. I think what he provided the Browns is somewhat overlooked because he was one of the very best running backs in the league. He was overshadowed by Brian Sipe and the passing game, but that passing game wouldn't have been as effective as it was without Pruitt drawing so much attention with his running abilities."

"Mike was a power running back and had the ability to feel his way across the line of scrimmage and find where the open spots were," Paul Warfield said. "Essentially, I saw him as a power running back but with great, explosive initial speed and certainly having the competitive edge to become an outstanding player, which he developed into."

"He was just a shade below Earl Campbell. I thought he was that type of back," said Joe DeLamielleure. "He had breakaway speed and he was powerful. He was a real threat because he could catch, too. He was good."

"I liked the way Pruitt played," said Jeff Schudel. "He did the hard work. He was a bullish guy. He'd break tackles, pick up the tough yards. He was a really good receiver, too. He was the heart of that team in the era that he played."

Kevin Mack resembled appropriately a Mack Truck when he was running with the football. He was a powerful back but also had great speed.

"He was a load," said Peticca. "What was really remarkable was at times he demonstrated breakaway speed. I'm not sure, for whatever reason, the Browns ever got as much out of him as was there. But he made a lot of plays that were really big that people don't remember only because he was getting four yards on third-and-three or he was running for a first down with three minutes left and a three-point lead. He wasn't known for

Kevin Mack running with the football (JERRY COLI/DREAMSTIME.COM)

the flashy 30-yard play that everyone remembers. He made the plays you have to have to win games and preserve wins. He was probably one of the best in the league in making those key, little short-yardage runs that you had to have."

"Kevin was one of those guys who ran so slow that I don't think people realized how fast he was, kind of like Nick Chubb," said Doug Dieken. "Guys would take the wrong angle because he ran so smooth that you'd be watching him, and the next thing they knew he'd be by them because they took the wrong angle."

"Kevin was a quiet guy but was a good, powerful runner," Mike McLain said.

"He would literally take opponents into the end zone on his back," said Schudel. "He played hard and was a very humble guy."

Mack immediately hit it off with Earnest Byner in Mack's rookie season of 1985. His relationship with Byner was pretty special. "We just kind of latched onto each other and challenged each other, too," he said. "Of course, there were things he could do that I couldn't do, but there were also things I could do that he couldn't do. It kind of sparked a little bit of a rivalry as far as trying to accomplish things, just to outdo the other guy. I think that helped us as players, helped us to kind of reach our peaks, or at least helped us get there."

Mack will always be proud of he and Byner both rushing for 1,000 yards in 1985. "It was really cool because Earnest and I were pretty much unknown guys," he said. "For us to perform like we did was really special for us. We were a little one-dimensional, but we always seemed to go out and make it work, and I think we took pride in that. Even though people knew we were a run-heavy team, we went out and said, 'Okay, you guys know we're coming, so stop us.'"

Mack missed most of the 1989 season when he was arrested for drug trafficking, for which he served a month in jail and spent another month in rehab. He returned to the Browns in early December that season, and in a Saturday night showdown for the AFC Central title in the season finale at Houston, he carried his team on his back on a late drive that resulted in his game-winning 4-yard touchdown run. After all that had happened to him that season, the moment was very special.

"It was really great to know that the Browns gave me a second chance," Mack said. "I was kind of trying to repay the team for what it'd been through with me, which was tough, not just for me but also for the team."

Mack will always fondly remember playing in front of Browns fans. "Browns fans are pretty much the same as Clemson fans," he said. "When I think of Browns fans, it immediately takes me back to Clemson. And both teams wear orange! Playing for the Browns in that stadium really felt like a college atmosphere. It would get so loud in there, it was unbelievable. And when it got loud, it would vibrate."

HALFBACK

THE CANDIDATES

Bobby Mitchell
Ernie Green
Leroy Kelly
Greg Pruitt
Earnest Byner

The Browns had some decent halfbacks in the late 1940s and early 1950s, one of whom was Edgar "Special Delivery" Jones. Jones played for Cleveland from 1946 to 1949. His rushing yardage totals from 1946 to 1948 were, respectively, 539, 443, and 400. In 1948, he had 14 receptions for 293 yards with five touchdowns.

Dub Jones played for the Browns from 1948 to 1955. His best season was 1951 when he rushed for 492 yards with seven touchdowns and had 30 receptions for 570 yards with five touchdowns. That year, on November 25 in a 42–21 victory over the Chicago Bears, he tied an NFL record by scoring six touchdowns. The next season, he caught 43 passes for 651 yards with four touchdowns. He was First-Team All-Pro in 1951 and a Pro Bowler in 1951 and 1952.

Coming aboard in 1958 as a seventh-round draft choice from the University of Illinois was Bobby Mitchell. Mitchell had a nice four seasons with the Browns from 1958 to 1961. He was second on the team behind Jim Brown in rushing yards in each of those years. His rushing yardage totals, respectively, were 500, 743, 506, and 548. He scored 16 rushing touchdowns with the Browns, including a 90-yarder in a 31–17 victory over Washington on November 15, 1959. He could also catch passes out of the backfield. His receptions/receiving yardage totals in his last three years with Cleveland were, respectively, 35/351, 45/612, and 32/368. He totaled 16 touchdown catches with the Browns. Mitchell was a Pro Bowler in 1960. He was traded to the Redskins after the 1961 season. He was switched to wide receiver in DC and went on to a Hall of Fame career, getting inducted in 1983.

Ernie Green did a fine job at halfback from 1963 to 1965. He was switched to fullback in 1966 and 1967, his two Pro Bowl years, with Jim Brown retired and Leroy Kelly as the halfback. In 1966, Green rushed for 750 yards with three touchdowns and had 45 receptions for 445 yards with six touchdowns. The next season, he ran for 710 yards with four touchdowns and caught 39 passes for 369 yards with two touchdowns.

Kelly, meanwhile, was off and running to a career that would get him inducted into the Pro Football Hall of Fame in 1994. He rushed for 1,141 yards and a league-leading 15 touchdowns in 1966. In 1967, he had an NFL-leading 1,205 yards on the ground with a league-best 11 touchdowns. The next year, he led the NFL with both 1,239 yards rushing and 16 rushing touchdowns. He was the Browns' leader in rushing yards every season from 1966 to 1972. He was First-Team All-Pro from 1966 to 1968 and a Pro Bowler from 1966 to 1971.

Greg Pruitt led the Browns in rushing yards each season from 1974 to 1978. He rushed for at least 1,000 yards in 1975, 1976, and 1977, and nearly gained 1,000 rushing yards in 1978. He suffered an injury in a 1979 game at St. Louis, which ended

Leroy Kelly running with the football against St. Louis early in his career
(PAUL TEPLEY/CLEVELAND STATE UNIVERSITY CLEVELAND PRESS ARCHIVES)

his season. He was fantastic as a receiver out of the backfield also, with his best years coming in 1980 (50 receptions) and 1981 (65 receptions). He was a Pro Bowler in 1973, 1974, 1976, and 1977.

The next great Cleveland halfback was Earnest Byner. His best season on the ground was in 1985 when he had 1,002 yards with eight touchdowns. That year, he also had 45 receptions for 460 yards with two touchdowns. He had eight rushing touchdowns in 1987. His best receiving season with the Browns was 1988 when he caught 59 passes for 576 yards with two touchdowns. Byner was even better in the postseason. In a 24–21 loss at Miami in a divisional playoff on January 4, 1986, he rushed for 161 yards with two touchdowns and had four receptions for 25 yards. In a 38–21 victory over the Colts in a divisional playoff on January 9, 1988, he rushed for 122 yards with a touchdown and caught four passes for 36 yards with a score. The next week, in a 38–33 loss at Denver in the AFC championship, he had seven receptions for 120 yards with a touchdown and rushed for 67 yards with a touchdown.

In the running for best Browns halfback ever are Mitchell, Green, Kelly, Pruitt, and Byner.

BOBBY MITCHELL

Bobby Mitchell was the ultimate player for what Paul Brown wanted when it came to speed.

"Mitchell was the perfect complement to Jim Brown, and Jim Brown would tell you that," said Steve King. "They were perfect complements for one another. Jim Brown said, 'With all due respect to Ernie Davis, we were two big backs. We would've been much more effective had we kept Bobby Mitchell.' Mitchell had no ego either. He would've been happy to stay with the Browns as Jim Brown's sidekick."

Mitchell was one of the early speed players who came into the NFL. "We, of course, used him primarily as a running back with the sweeps and chips and all of that," John Wooten said.

"Bobby was a great one," said Jim Ray Smith.

ERNIE GREEN

Ernie Green did not mind playing second banana. With Jim Brown and later Leroy Kelly as Cleveland's main running backs, he pretty much had no choice.

"Football is a team sport," he said, "and as long as everybody is doing their assigned jobs, the likelihood of success is quite good. I was really determined to do whatever I could to contribute to the success of the team. Whatever the other guy's skill sets were, I could do those things that he was not good at. And, as a result, I ended up being 'the other guy' who did 'the other stuff.'

"While I was growing up, the game was a team sport and a team game, and we all had to contribute. And I took a lot of pride in doing what I was taught to do and helping my teams win. I was taught to play that way, and it was my responsibility to do what I was asked to do, and I did it with everything in my being."

"Ernie certainly was a monumental player as far as I'm concerned," said Paul Warfield. "No one on that football team gave more of himself, sacrificed more, and put aside what he possibly could've done individually to just be a part of a team and to help the Cleveland Browns win. He had the unenviable task of being in the same backfield as Jim because, if you had Jim in the backfield, if you're running the ball four times, three out of the four times Jim was going to run it. Every running back wants to run the football, and Ernie was more than capable of doing that, but his number one assignment was to be the lead blocker for Jim. And he did that to perfection."

When Brown retired suddenly during the summer of 1966, the Browns were obviously concerned. "It kind of set us back a little bit," said Green in the November 2004 *Bernie's Insiders*. "But Leroy Kelly was ready to play. I was still healthy and ready to play. We had the potential to do quite well. Opposing teams couldn't key on anyone because if they keyed on Kelly, I would get away. And if they keyed on me, Kelly would get away. But if they were keying on Jim Brown 90 percent of the time, they were right. And that's why it was a great [1966] season for the two of us and the team."

"I think Green was probably always underrated among the fans simply because he was next to Brown and then Kelly. He probably had the ability to be the featured back," Mike Peticca said. "He was a tough between-the-tackles runner who could also get outside and break a big run. He had the well-deserved reputation as an excellent pass catcher, too, and even more as a terrific blocker. He was one of those guys who, just because of his abilities, made everybody else better."

"He, like Leroy, could run the ball inside, slide outside, had great instincts of running skills, but also like Leroy, he was an outstanding pass receiver out of the backfield," said Warfield. "He and Leroy gave us more diversity. Teams had to defend us in different ways."

Green was an outstanding, skilled running back who could run the ball, catch the ball, and was an outstanding blocker. "He was the most selfless running back you'd ever see," said John Wooten.

"Ernie was one of the most unselfish players I've ever seen," Dick Schafrath said. "He was special."

"He was an unsung hero," said Ray Yannucci.

LEROY KELLY

Ray Yannucci will never forget going to Hiram College in the summer of 1964 to watch a rookie by the name of Paul Warfield practice.

"I saw this guy returning punts," he said. "I didn't know who he was, thinking to myself, 'Who's this number 44?' I looked at my friend and said, 'There's the next great running back for the Cleveland Browns.'"

As it turned out, it was another rookie by the name of Leroy Kelly. "You could just see the way he ran and his moves," continued Yannucci. "He was amazing."

"I went to an exhibition game that 1964 season against the Steelers at the Rubber Bowl," laughed Mike Peticca. "The Browns had a backup running back named Ken Webb. Sometime in the second half, Leroy Kelly goes on to the field and I said to my dad, 'Who's this guy Kelly? I want to see Ken Webb!'"

During his first two seasons, Kelly was relegated mainly to kick return duties. When Jim Brown retired, Kelly got his shot.

He would be the starting halfback, while Ernie Green would switch from halfback to fullback.

"I knew Leroy Kelly was a star," said Brown. "In fact, I wrote a letter to Blanton Collier and told him that. I knew he was good. He was a hell of a runner, no doubt about it. I knew he would fill in beautifully, and I had no intentions of sticking around and trying to keep him out of the lineup, or play longer than I should've. He's in the Hall of Fame, and he did an unbelievable job."

"Blanton told me, 'This is your opportunity to be the starter,'" said Kelly. "That was my chance. That's fate, destiny. And I took advantage of it."

Kelly knew he belonged in the Browns' backfield in the very first game of the 1966 season against the Washington Redskins. "I scored on a 29-yard run off the left side," he said. "After that game I said, 'Well, I think I have arrived. This is going to be nice, I like this.'"

"We were fortunate to have Leroy waiting in the wings to take his rightful place to keep the team as a contender for league championships," said Paul Warfield. "The success of the Cleveland Browns still was at an extremely high level. Leroy, along with Gale Sayers of the Bears, were perhaps the two best running backs in the NFL during a span of several years."

Kelly's running style was one in which he could certainly get the integral tough yardage, short yardage, but he could run plays for 30 or more yards as well. He was explosive and very versatile, too. He could come out of the backfield and work in intermediate areas of the field against linebackers who found it very difficult to cover him. "In a manner of speaking," Warfield continued, "certainly that factored into my ability to work certain areas of the field in which coverages started to change against me and more double coverage was implemented. And that would put linebackers one on one with Leroy. His versatility showed up because we utilized a pass play in which Leroy would take a quick pitch, go to his left, stop, turn, and throw the ball to me downfield, so that presented multiple problems for defensive units. It gave us another dimension, his ability to throw the football, and throw it accurately, and team up with me, which not only helped me but helped our offense significantly."

"Kelly," Peticca added, "was one of my favorite players simply because he was so great in what initially seemed like such an underdog role—having to replace Jim Brown. You remember him in those quick bursts right off the snap and his shiftiness. It seemed like tacklers seldom got a full hit on him. And, of course, he made lots of big plays as a receiver."

"Leroy was pretty good at gaining yards. He was explosive," said Fred Hoaglin. "The thing that I remember so much about him was when we were in the huddle and the game was close, I can't ever remember him saying anything, but you could tell he wanted the ball so bad. His nostrils would flare, almost like a bull. He was the most intense guy in the huddle. He wanted the ball when the game was on the line because he knew that he could do the job, and we did too. We wanted him to have the ball."

"Leroy was amazing. He had the quickest start in the league," said Dan Coughlin. "In fact, the Browns' coaches always had to caution the referee, telling him, 'Be careful, you're gonna be tempted to flag him for motion.' His first step was so quick, it fooled you."

"Kelly went on to gain the reputation of a great 'bad-field' runner," Peticca said. "I remember people calling him a 'mudder' because he was so great on those 'bad-track' fields."

"Leroy had the quickness and speed, and could change direction so fast, to be able to break a play from anywhere on the field," said John Wooten. "He was also one of the quietest, most humble superstars I've ever known."

"After about three or four years, Blanton Collier named him co-captain!" Coughlin recalled. "You'd think a captain would have to be a little more of a vocal guy, but not Leroy. He led by example."

GREG PRUITT

Leroy Kelly's final season of 1973 was Greg Pruitt's rookie year. And Pruitt did a wonderful job of carrying on the great running back tradition of the Browns—but not before he had to learn an early lesson from the veteran.

"At first I thought to myself, 'I finished second in the Heisman voting [his senior year of 1972], I'm just as good as Leroy Kelly and any other back here,'" Pruitt recalled. "But soon I realized Leroy had been in the pros a long time and knew a whole lot more than me, like some of the intricacies of the game. I started to listen to him."

"Greg really believed that he should've gotten the Heisman, and I think he carried that chip on his shoulder throughout his career," said Ray Yannucci. "He was probably one of the best running backs the Browns have ever had. He could run inside, outside, he could catch passes out of the backfield. He was a cocky guy, and I say that as a compliment. That's what helped make him good. He had a hell of a career."

Pruitt had an amusing experience after a critical win over Pittsburgh at Municipal Stadium on November 25 of his rookie season. He scored on a 19-yard run with less than a minute left in the game for what turned out to be the winning touchdown. Thousands of fans rushed the field when the clock hit 0:00.

"You would've thought we just won a championship," Pruitt remembered. "It was then that I realized just what the rivalry with the Steelers means to Browns fans, how important it is. It was really something, the way those fans went crazy. It reminded me of my days at Oklahoma, where football is like a religion. I had thousands of people hitting me, slapping me, on the helmet. It was nuts! I was able to get to the dugout and into the tunnel. I figured once I got into the locker room, there would be a whole lot of press and media people wanting to interview me and ask me questions. So while I was walking to the locker room, I was planning out what I was going to say."

When Pruitt opened the door to the locker room, he was in for quite a surprise. It was the Pittsburgh Steelers' locker room! "I went to the wrong locker room!" he exclaimed. "Chuck Noll was screaming at his players. When I walked in, it got so quiet you could hear a pin drop. I got out of there pretty fast."

He headed back toward the field.

"The fans were still out there, though," he recalled. "On one end of the tunnel were thousands of fans going berserk, and on the other end was the Steelers' locker room. I was stuck! So I just stood in the tunnel, waiting for the fans to leave."

The press was gone by the time Pruitt got to the Browns' locker room.

Pruitt was a big threat in many ways. He could break a run at any time and was a terrific receiver. "He was the one link to greatness that the Browns had in '74 and '75 when the roster had become so old or was filled with journeyman players," Mike Peticca said. "He had to be one of the most fun players to watch, not the way he broke the big runs but the aesthetics of how it happened, his various moves, his ability to change direction and change pace. I'll never forget that Cincinnati game in '75 when the 0-9 Browns upset the 8-1 Bengals. What a spectacular game by Pruitt. That set the whole country on notice of what a great player he was."

Pruitt was a legitimate thousand-yard rusher who was versatile, explosive, and could take a handoff and go the distance. "He could make the vital, necessary yards you would need," said Paul Warfield. "He could hurt defenses with his running ability, which was outstanding because he was what you would call a long-ball runner. But he also had the ability to go out of the backfield because he was a very adept receiver working on linebackers on the strong or weak side of the formation. He was a mismatch for them."

For the first handful of seasons of Pruitt's career, he made famous the tear-away jersey, which helped him gain a few more yards here and there. "I personally did not like the tear-away," he said. "More and more people realized that I wore it and understood that I played a big part of the offense, that I was a primary receiver, or primary person, that the Browns went

Greg Pruitt trying to elude Pittsburgh's Jack Lambert (58) and "Mean Joe" Greene in 1975 (MALCOLM W. EMMONS/WIKIMEDIA COMMONS)

to in key situations, and they would just tear my jersey off and tell the referee. I'd have to leave the field to put a new jersey on. So I found myself running to and from the sideline more than I liked, and I couldn't really get into the flow of the game. One time, before a game with the Dallas Cowboys, I was walking out of the tunnel with [Cowboys receiver] Bob Hayes. He said, 'Hey, is that a tear-away you got on?' He walked up and tore it off! And he said, 'Oh, I guess it is.' I had to turn around and go back to the locker room and change my jersey."

The tear-away jersey, which was banned in the NFL because of Pruitt in 1979, enhanced Pruitt's style, but he did alright without it. "Every time he touched the ball, you always felt something big was going to happen," said Mike McLain. "He was one of the truly big-play running backs in team history."

"He was kind of flashy, and he was such a quick guy with those slick moves," Jeff Schudel added.

"When I first got to Cleveland, I was always impressed with Greg because I used to watch him in college," said Mike Pruitt, his running mate for several years. "I always thought he had some moves! Him having the moves he had and me doing what I could do from a power-back standpoint, it worked out perfectly."

"Greg Pruitt could catch the ball as well as any back in the league," Reggie Rucker said.

Recalled Dan Coughlin, "Greg once said, 'They can weigh a guy, they can measure him, they can time him, but they can't measure what kind of a heart he has.'"

"What a shame that he hurt his knee in '79," said Peticca. "I think he was a Hall of Fame-caliber talent. If he had been healthy a couple more years, we might've seen that become a reality."

EARNEST BYNER

The Fumble.

Earnest Byner will always be linked to that play toward the end of the 1987 AFC Championship Game in Denver. And that is unfortunate.

"It was a simple trap play," said Byner. "I bounced outside and pulled the ball in to protect it but not up and across like I should have. I wasn't even looking at Jeremiah Castille; he wasn't going to get me. I was focusing on the other safety, Tony Lilly."

That is a shame because Castille wound up stripping the ball from Byner and recovering it. "It was one of the low points of, not only my football life, but my *life*," Byner continued. "I felt like I let everyone down—teammates, fans, coaches."

On the other hand, Byner believes that game was one of the most thrilling of his career. "We were down, 21–3, at the half," he said. "But we never felt like we were out of it. We kept plugging away. We were moving the ball. They couldn't stop us. We focus on the negative sometimes in society. I got lots of letters from fans lambasting me like I was *trying* to fumble. On the other end, there was a hell of a lot of support from fans and teammates."

That is because the Browns would not have even been in the position to tie the game late in the fourth quarter without Byner. He had one heck of a game, amassing 120 yards receiving on seven receptions with a touchdown and 67 yards rushing on 15 carries with a score.

"After the play, I think there were just too many guys trying to console Earnest at the time, so I just kind of laid back and waited until me and him had the opportunity to be alone," said Kevin Mack. "And I probably didn't say much more than the other guys said to him, like it wasn't his fault, he played his heart out, and if it wasn't for him we wouldn't have been in the position we were in."

For most of his rookie season in 1984, Byner was used mainly as a kickoff returner and coverage man on special teams. Then Marty Schottenheimer replaced Sam Rutigliano at the season's halfway point, and things changed. "Marty told me I'm his guy," Byner said. "I knew only one way to play, and that was full speed. I think Marty liked that."

Byner gave the coaching staff something to ponder during the offseason by rushing for 188 yards in a season-ending win at Houston. "My tendency in the pros was always to get stronger towards the end of each year," he said.

"What a great surprise he was as the '84 season wound down," said Mike Peticca. "He established himself right away as a legitimate and special NFL talent. He was a great big-game player. I think that's one of the reasons people felt bad for him with The Fumble because sometimes that one play tends to overshadow a body of work over a whole career. I know it's cliché, but the Browns are out of that Denver game if not for Byner's remarkable efforts. The season before, in '86, he dealt with a lot of injuries and didn't play a lot. Who knows what would've happened if he'd really been healthy that year? He was a very good blocker and demonstrated what a good receiver he was. His attitude, his competitiveness, if you're playing with him, I have to believe were contagious."

Nobody played with more heart and was more of a fan favorite because of how hard he played than Byner. He was more talented than his defensive counterpart, linebacker Eddie Johnson. Everybody loved Johnson because he played hard. Byner was Johnson but with a lot more ability. "You talk about guys who are willing to take one for the team," Steve King said. "Byner also developed into a great pass receiver when Lindy Infante came in as the offensive coordinator in 1986. And that's what a great player does. When you're part of a team, you do what is asked and he did it, never cried about it, never complained about it. And it helped the team because Byner and Kevin Mack ended up being the perfect complement where you had all those receivers. Rutigliano said of Byner during the '94 training camp, 'He pushes the pile.' And he did. He just would not stop. He was a tremendous player."

"Earnest was a tough guy. He ran with authority," said Doug Dieken. "But he also had the ability to lead a defender. If the guy was going to come up and 'stone' him, he'd put a move on and the guy would miss. If the guy came up and was going to come right at him, Earnest would run right over him. He was a powerful guy and had good hands, too, for a running back. He gave Bernie [Kosar] a lot of options out of the backfield."

Byner was traded to Washington after the 1988 season but returned to the Browns in 1994 and played with them through 1995. He will never forget the last home game of the 1995 season against the Bengals, which turned out to be the last home game for four years due to Art Modell moving the Browns to Baltimore after the season.

"I witnessed a lot of tears," Byner said. "You couldn't have written a book any better. After the game I told Tony Jones, 'I'm gonna go over to the fans.' And I did, and Tony came with me, and then many of our teammates followed. We went around the whole stadium shaking hands with, and hugging, the fans. It was a good ride in Cleveland, especially the first time around."

"Earnest Byner was probably one of the most talented overachievers the NFL has ever seen," said Ray Yannucci. "If you go back and look where he was drafted, very low [10th round], he probably shouldn't even have made the team. But he was a very self-confident, mentally tough guy, and a really, really solid person, a great person. I really believe that, during the Marty-Bernie era, Earnest Byner was the heart and soul of the Cleveland Browns."

AND THE WINNER IS . . .

Bobby Mitchell did not turn into a Hall of Fame player until the Browns traded him to the Redskins, where he became a wide receiver. That does not mean, however, that he did not have a fine four seasons with Cleveland. As Jim Brown's sidekick, he produced some fine rushing statistics and also some very good receiving numbers, the latter foreshadowing his days with Washington.

Ernie Green played alongside Jim Brown and then Leroy Kelly in the Browns' backfield for his entire career. He was still able to have some pretty decent statistics, though. He was a solid halfback beside Brown and a solid fullback alongside Kelly.

Who knows what would have happened to Kelly had Jim Brown not retired before the 1966 season? He may have stayed a kick returner for his entire career. But Brown *did* retire, and Kelly shined in his new spotlight, leading the NFL in rushing yards in both 1967 and 1968 and in rushing touchdowns each season from 1966 to 1968.

Greg Pruitt was *the* man on offense for the Browns in the mid- to late 1970s. He was one of the fastest halfbacks in the NFL, and he was magnificent as a receiver out of the backfield. He had nagging injuries throughout his career, but when he hurt himself against the Cardinals in 1979, not only did it end his season, it ended his great days as a rusher. From that point on with Cleveland, he was mostly used as a receiver out of the backfield. He put up stellar receiving numbers in 1980 and 1981, his last two seasons with the Browns.

Earnest Byner was a talented halfback in his seven seasons with the Browns. He was a good runner and receiver who also had a lot of heart and got just about everything out of his talents that God gave him. He nearly by himself got the 8-8 Browns to hosting—yes, hosting!—the AFC Championship Game in 1985 with his masterful performance against the heavily favored Dolphins in the divisional playoffs. He almost got the Browns into Super Bowl XXII with his sensational performances in the playoffs that 1987 season.

When all is said and done, the choice for greatest Browns halfback ever is **Leroy Kelly**.

HALFBACKS WHO DID NOT MAKE THE CUT

Edgar "Special Delivery" Jones always seemed to deliver.

"They called him 'Six Yards Special Delivery' Jones because he ran for six yards so many times," said Bob Dolgan. "He was a very strong runner, a very hardnosed runner."

"Edgar Jones was a very good player," Steve King said. "He would've blossomed other places. When he was called upon, he played very well, no doubt about it."

Dub Jones was a running back, he was a receiver, he could do it all.

"He was the most complete player the Browns had," said King. "But because you had Dante Lavelli and Mac Speedie and because you had Marion Motley, you didn't need a guy to be anything else other than being able to do both—run with the ball and catch the ball. Jones could fit into any offense. He was just a great player.

"Edgar Jones and Dub Jones would've been the central part of the offense had they played anywhere else other than Cleveland. Because they played for the Browns, there were one or two things they were asked to do, and they did them. You subjugate personal gain for the good of the team, and both of those guys did that."

"Those two are probably some of the best players the Cleveland Browns have ever produced," Ray Yannucci said.

TACKLES

Lou Groza
Mike McCormack
Dick Schafrath
Joe Thomas

Lou Groza may have been nicknamed "The Toe," but he was probably a better left tackle than he was a kicker. And that is saying a lot. From 1946 to 1959, he helped pave the way for such running backs as Marion Motley, Bobby Mitchell, and Jim Brown. He protected Otto Graham's blind side. And he did both jobs very well. He was First-Team All-Pro from 1952 to 1955 and was a Pro Bowler from 1950 to 1955 and 1957 to 1959. He was inducted into the Pro Football Hall of Fame as a tackle in 1974.

Mike McCormack was a stalwart at right tackle for the Browns from 1955 to 1962 after playing middle guard in 1954. He blocked for Mitchell and Brown. He was voted to the Pro Bowl in 1956 and 1957 and from 1960 to 1962. He was enshrined into the Pro Football Hall of Fame in 1984.

Taking over for Groza as Cleveland's starting left tackle in 1960 and staying there through 1971 was Dick Schafrath. Schafrath carried on the torch at that position quite well. He was First-Team All-Pro from 1963 to 1965 and in 1969. He was a Pro Bowler from 1963 to 1968.

Manning the starting right tackle position for the Browns from 1963 to 1969, Monte Clark helped create holes for Brown and Leroy Kelly to burst through. He helped protect Frank Ryan and Bill Nelsen.

Replacing Schafrath at left tackle in 1971, Doug Dieken blocked for Kelly, Greg Pruitt, and Mike Pruitt. He helped protect Brian Sipe. He was a Pro Bowler in 1980.

Cody Risien was Cleveland's starting right tackle from 1980 to 1983 and 1985 to 1989 after spending his rookie season in 1979 playing left guard. He blocked for the two Pruitts, Earnest Byner, and Kevin Mack. He helped protect Sipe and Bernie Kosar. He was a Pro Bowler in 1986 and 1987. He missed the 1984 season due to a knee injury suffered in the final preseason game at Philadelphia.

Playing mainly left tackle for the Browns from 1988 to 1995, Tony Jones did his job very well. He never played in a Pro Bowl with Cleveland, but he was considered one of the better left tackles in the league. He blocked for Byner, Mack, and Eric Metcalf and helped protect Kosar.

Joe Thomas is a sure Hall of Famer. First ballot? Perhaps. He played left tackle for the Browns from 2007 to 2017. Unfortunately, he played on only one team that had a winning record, in his rookie year. He paved the way for running backs Jamal Lewis, Jerome Harrison, Peyton Hillis, and Isaiah Crowell. He holds the unofficial NFL record of playing on 10,363 consecutive snaps. Thomas was First-Team All-Pro from 2009 to 2011 and 2013 to 2015. He was voted to the Pro Bowl every season but his last.

Starting every game for the Browns at right tackle from 2012 to 2015, Mitchell Schwartz was one of the best in the league in his time with Cleveland. He blocked for Crowell, Trent Richardson, and Terrance West.

The tackles in the running for best ever in Browns history are Groza, McCormack, Schafrath, and Thomas.

LOU GROZA

Lou Groza was one of the best left tackles of all time. Period.

"Before they called it what it is today, protecting the quarterback's blind side, that's what Lou Groza did for Otto Graham," said Steve King. "You look at Graham. He didn't get beat up, he didn't get sacked. He stayed healthy, upright, and that was Lou Groza."

"Lou was an outstanding offensive tackle," said John Wooten.

"Lou was awesome," Fred Hoaglin said. "He was like a father figure to everybody on the team when I was there."

"He was good," recalled Jim Ray Smith. "He kind of took me under his wing when I went to Cleveland."

Said Ray Yannucci, "He's an icon among everyone who has ever played for the Cleveland Browns."

MIKE MCCORMACK

Mike McCormack may not be one of the first players who comes to mind when the discussion is Browns Hall of Famers, but he should be. He was that good.

"When was the first time you really heard about a right tackle with greatness? It was Mike McCormack," said Steve King. "He was a great player, an unbelievable player. He was as good at right tackle as Lou Groza was at left tackle. Because Groza was the kicker and was the left tackle, the latter which was, even back then, a key position, Groza got more attention."

"Mike was tough, one of the best to ever play the game at the tackle position," John Wooten said. "He was also a great leader, an outstanding leader."

DICK SCHAFRATH

Dick Schafrath weighed 220 pounds as a rookie in 1959. In his second season the next year, he was up to 270 pounds.

"I started weightlifting, and I was the biggest guy on the team for about six, seven years," he said. "Paul Brown was mad at me because he didn't believe in weightlifting. He hated it. He liked you to run, run, run and thought weightlifting would tighten you up too much. He accepted it, though, and left me alone because I was doing my job."

Schafrath was always undersized for a tackle, so, in addition to his weightlifting, he had to eat a lot. "That's how he developed this ravenous appetite," said Dan Coughlin. "He could eat like nobody on the team because he had to keep building up his size."

Schafrath was in awe right from the start on the football field. "The first huddle I was in," he recalled, "there were nine future Hall of Famers. So you had a lot of expectations when you stepped in a huddle like that. Lou Groza took me under his wing, along with Mike McCormack."

According to Schafrath, with Paul Brown, you normally blocked a guy and just stayed with him and tried to drive him in the ground. You pretty much stayed with your man no matter what. "But that wasn't enough when you played under Blanton Collier in his first three years as head coach, which were Jim Brown's last three," he said. "It was everybody hit. We called it option-blocking. Once Jimmy would see you start with your hit on one side or the other of a guy, as soon as you hit him, you didn't stay with him another two seconds. You tried to go past him and get a second block because Jim Brown didn't mess around—he was goin'. On that offensive line, we had it going that some guys were getting two blocks, and three blocks at times, on the same play. It became an obsession with the offensive line to make more than one block. Jimmy always says that it was fun to run with that group because, every time he would turn another direction or spin out of a block, there were two or three more guys coming again. It was this wave of us coming and knocking guys down and getting up again and going again. Hell, even Gary Collins and Paul Warfield were sixth and seventh guys blocking!"

"Dick Schafrath and Gene Hickerson, along with all the members of that offensive line, were essentially vital," Warfield said, "because, going into every ballgame, I'm sure that the opposing teams wanted to, as a part of their defensive game plans, stop the run of the Cleveland Browns with Jim Brown and then his successor, Leroy Kelly. There was Ernie Green, too. We were, in those years, a run-oriented football team, which meant we needed to have an outstanding offensive line. Dick Schafrath was a very good player who, I believe initially when he joined the Browns, was a little bit undersized as far as physical weight is concerned and had to develop and gain more weight to become an offensive tackle in the National Football League, which he worked very diligently at and became that. He became a Pro Bowl performer. Playing at the left tackle position, usually the best defensive rushers come from that side of the line. That meant he had to play and execute in the run game as well as the passing game. He was an outstanding offensive tackle."

"Schafrath should be in the Hall of Fame, and then you've got two guys in Monte Clark and John Wooten who may not be as recognized but approached greatness themselves," said Mike Peticca. "The Packers' sweep back then with halfback Paul Hornung and fullback Jim Taylor running the ball is the one that people look back on, but all you've got to do is look at the numbers to know the Browns' sweep was just as good, or better, than the Packers'. And it shows, obviously, with what Jim Brown and Ernie Green, and later Leroy Kelly and Green, accomplished running the ball. The line was also very good in protecting the passer.

"Schafrath's enthusiasm, too, I think fans really appreciated. Nowadays, there are all these celebrations and dances after any little thing that happens. Back then, a guy would score a touchdown, the team would run off the field, and the guys would shake hands as they got to the sidelines. But Schafrath would always sprint towards the guy who scored the touchdown and jump on him or hug him. There was a real enthusiastic thing that was unique in those days, and that was fun to watch."

"You hear people talk about how players make themselves great players. That was Dick," said Wooten. "Nobody worked harder. He was a bulldog type of a guy. He was undersized but just fought you to the bitter, bitter end. If you ever got into a fight, you'd want him on your side."

Schafrath loved playing in front of the hometown crowd.

"The difference then," he said, "was you really had a good relationship with the fans because you parked in the parking lot with them and walked with them to the stadium 100 yards, and everybody was signing autographs and taking pictures with you. The fans really were in very close contact with you, so it was like the whole family experience. That stadium was something to play in . . . wow!"

JOE THOMAS

Steve King will never forget his first impression of Joe Thomas.

"In the first 10 minutes of rookie minicamp in 2007, the year Thomas was drafted, all of the media people were standing there," he recalled. "We're looking from the waist up, how he moves and all of that. I noticed Doug Dieken was looking down. I finally said to Dieken, 'What are you looking at?' He said, 'This kid has great feet, really good feet. He has a chance to make it.' Dieken is smarter than the rest of us, so he sees what Joe Thomas was going to be 10 minutes into his first practice. And he was right on point. Thomas was a wonderful technician. He never let the Browns and their losing ways affect the way he prepared for the game and played the game. He was a pro's pro."

Thomas had great technique and was a smart guy. He was what you wanted in a textbook left tackle, a player who could block anybody be it speed or power and a guy who did not make mistakes. "He didn't get many holding penalties in his career," said Dieken, "and he never seemed to get into trouble. He was as solid as you could get."

"I think his consecutive-snaps streak pretty much says it all," Mike McLain said. "To play that position for that long, to me it's a better streak than Cal Ripken's streak. I may be thrown into baseball hell for that. Thomas was a Hall of Fame tackle, a great technician, but the endurance was like nothing I've ever seen."

"He never missed a snap until he was injured," added Jeff Schudel. "His feet were so quick, and he was such a technician that I will be very surprised if he doesn't end up in the Hall of Fame. Maybe not first ballot, but certainly the first couple years he's eligible."

And the Winners Are . . .

The Browns' headquarters rests on **Lou Groza** Boulevard in Berea.

Enough said.

Groza meant so much to the Browns franchise even if he had not been a kicker in addition to his left tackle duties. As a left tackle, he began the great tradition at that position for

Cleveland that would continue for years. He has one spot for the best tackles in Browns history.

Dick Schafrath once canoed across Lake Erie. He once ran from Cleveland all the way to Wooster. He even wrestled a bear! Playing left tackle in the NFL was nothing compared to those endeavors. Schafrath dominated opposing defensive linemen who were trying to get to the quarterback, and he dominated opposing defensive linemen who were attempting to get to the ball-carrier. The fact that he is not in the Pro Football Hall of Fame is a disgrace. He takes the other spot for best Browns tackles of all time.

TACKLES WHO DID NOT MAKE THE CUT

Quite simply, **Monte Clark** was a tough competitor as a right tackle for the Browns.

"Monte played with some of the worst injuries I've ever seen," said Fred Hoaglin. "One time, he tore his bicep muscle loose from his elbow. It rolled up into his shoulder. They had to massage that thing down and then tape his arm up so they could get it back in place for the game. I'd never seen anything like that."

"He was a hardworking, determined guy who was going to play in this league and be a part of a championship team," said John Wooten.

"Clark was a big, strong guy," Mike Peticca added. "He was a terrific pass blocker and an excellent run blocker."

"I don't remember too many guys running over him," said Tom Melody.

Doug Dieken may not have been fancy or as technically sound as Joe Thomas, but he played hard and he played hurt.

"He was a better tackle, I think, than maybe some people perceive him," said Steve King.

"You might label Dieken as an overachiever, not a very high draft choice," said Ray Yannucci. "He was an overachiever based on the fact that he never played on the offensive line up until he got to the Browns. He came to the Browns as a tight end out of the University of Illinois and was a wide receiver in high school. He made that transition from tight end to offensive lineman very, very well. He became one of the best left tackles who the Browns have ever had. Doug was a very, very good player."

"Doug Dieken was a very fine offensive lineman," Paul Warfield said. "He played well for the Browns. He certainly was a leader of the offensive line. I had great respect for his ability, for what he could do. Playing on the left side of the offensive line, you always played against the top rushers in the league. He was always stable and was an outstanding team leader and outstanding teammate."

Dieken holds the NFL record for most consecutive starts by an offensive tackle with 194. If there was ever a pillar for an offensive lineman, it was Dieken. "He carried on the tradition of Groza and Schafrath at left tackle," said Peticca. "What was funny about Dieken was that the whistle would blow and there would be holding, and everybody would say, 'Dieken.' It was partly because of his good nature to accept that, but that wasn't necessarily true. He was a very, very good player. I wish he would've made more than one Pro Bowl because he was certainly deserving of it. I don't know if there would've ever been one person who questioned his efforts and dependability. There's a saying that goes, 'The greatest ability is availability.' That's what Dieken embodied, and did it very well."

The 1980 season was Dieken's lone Pro Bowl year. "It kind of shows how the voting goes," he said. "If you win, you've got a better chance of going to the Pro Bowl than if you lose. I mean, I played the season on kind of one leg. I had strained knee ligaments. By far, it wasn't the best season I ever had."

"Everybody thought Doug was too small to be a tackle, but he protected Brian Sipe probably better than any lineman we had at the time. He had good hands and kept people off of him. He did very well," said Mike Pruitt. "He had some little tricks up his sleeve."

"Doug was solid," said Joe DeLamielleure. "He was a good player. He was a finesse guy. He wasn't as physical as Cody Risien, but he was a good pass blocker. He was like the prototype left tackle."

Cody Risien was drafted as a tackle but was moved to left guard during rookie training camp in 1979. As the summer progressed, his reps increased.

"All of a sudden," he said, "I started really excelling at pass protection, something I didn't have to do a whole lot at Texas A&M. And that's the name of the game in the NFL. Run-blockers are a dime a dozen. You've got to be able to pass-block. I had good, quick feet and I just got it."

Risien saw little action until he was sent in to play left guard late in the first quarter in Week 6 in 1979 against defending Super Bowl champion Pittsburgh, sending the starstruck rookie into a state of disbelief. "It was surreal," he said. "I'm thinking, 'Oh my gosh, this is the Pittsburgh Steelers! I'm out here against L.C. Greenwood and Joe Greene and Jack Lambert!' I was like, 'Somebody pinch me, okay? This isn't real!'"

Risien credited playing between Dieken and center Tom DeLeone as a huge reason for his success as a rookie. "I learned a lot," he said. "It was a pretty safe place to start my NFL career, between those two guys. They were really good at helping me out and making sure I was doing the right things. The offensive line is generally a very tight-knit group anyway, kind of a team within a team. The success of any offensive line really is based on the whole line, how everybody plays."

In his second season Risien was switched to right tackle, where he remained the rest of his career. "Cody was a good player when he came into the league, but he turned into a great player," said King. "He was rock solid on that right side. He was a great run blocker. You look at that Browns-Denver '87 AFC Championship Game and all those holes that Earnest Byner was running through, especially on that last drive. That was Cody Risien. He drove Karl Mecklenburg halfway to Boulder, Colorado. Mecklenburg was completely out of every play. Risien was as good of a right tackle other than Mike McCormack the Browns have ever had. Was he the best right tackle in the game during his time? I think so. He was that good."

"He was a legitimate Pro Bowl caliber player," said Peticca. "It was apparent how much the Browns missed him in '84 when he got injured during the preseason. That was probably the first big blow in what turned out to be a disastrous season because the Browns lost a number of close games. You've got to believe Risien's absence had a huge impact and maybe his presence would've been the difference in some of those games. It was really a bad break for Paul McDonald. Risien protected his blind side."

"When we got Cody, I thought, 'Wow! This guy's tall, he's big, has big hands,'" Mike Pruitt said. "He was a lineman who you'd be happy to be running behind because he was very strong and would move people out of the way."

"Cody was consistent," said Joe DeLamielleure. "I don't ever remember him having a bad game or making mental mistakes."

There are some players who just fall through the cracks, go undrafted but then make quite a name for themselves in the NFL.

Tony Jones was one of those players.

Undrafted out of Western Carolina University, Jones had a solid eight-year career with Cleveland, the last six of which he started every single game.

"The Browns had a very good offensive line in the late '80s, but then they started having some injuries and here comes Tony Jones. Who the heck is Tony Jones?" recalled King. "They put him at left tackle after trying him at guard and right tackle. For those last five seasons of the original Browns, Jones was a great player. He was quick, agile, and he was never a guy who complained. You never saw a lot of penetration from his side of the line. He was rock solid as a left tackle. He was very good and was a guy who really came out of nowhere. He was a pro's pro."

When Jones made a mistake, which was not often, he took the blame. Remembered King, "Bernie Kosar got hit in the '93 season, and it was Tony Jones saying, 'It was our fault. We need to protect him better. We need to do a better job.'"

"I remember Jones as very efficient, dependable, and a gifted offensive lineman," Peticca said. "After some of the old stalwarts like Risien got a little older, there might've been a consensus that Jones was the Browns' best offensive lineman during the late '80s and early '90s. He was pretty quick and was certainly well above average as both a run blocker and pass blocker."

When the Browns allowed **Mitchell Schwartz** to go on to the free agent market after the 2015 season, it raised eyebrows from the East Side to the West Side of town.

"I still think that was one of the biggest mistakes the Browns made when they let Mitchell go in free agency," said Dieken. "Mitchell was very, very consistent. He was a smart guy."

"I'll never figure out why they let him go, especially at a time when their offensive line was awful," said Mike McLain. "He was a quiet, unassuming guy. When you talked to him, you thought he was too nice to be playing football, but it was a big mistake for the Browns letting him go."

"I think Schwartz was a lot better than what we all thought because the team was struggling," King added. "When the team is bad, sometimes players turn bad, but that didn't happen with Schwartz. He was a very good player for the Browns."

"The Browns never should've let him go," said Jeff Schudel. "Right tackle was a revolving door for several years after he left."

GUARDS

Lin Houston
Jim Ray Smith
Gene Hickerson
John Wooten

Lin Houston was the first great guard the Browns had on their team. He played right guard for them from 1946 to 1953. He helped pave the way for Marion Motley, Edgar Jones, and Dub Jones and helped protect Otto Graham.

Manning left guard for the Browns from 1950 to 1956 was Abe Gibron. Gibron, like Houston, was one of the first great guards in team annals. He was picked for the Pro Bowl from 1952 to 1955.

Jim Ray Smith played mostly left guard for Cleveland from 1956 to 1962. He was as solid as they come, getting voted First-Team All-Pro from 1959 to 1961 and getting picked for the Pro Bowl from 1958 to 1962.

It was long overdue when Gene Hickerson was finally inducted into the Pro Football Hall of Fame in 2007. The former right guard for the Browns from 1958 to 1960 and 1962 to 1973 (he missed the 1961 season due to a leg injury) was one of the best at his position in league history. He created holes for

Jim Brown and Leroy Kelly, and he helped protect Frank Ryan and Bill Nelsen. Hickerson was First-Team All-Pro from 1967 to 1969 and was picked for the Pro Bowl from 1965 to 1970.

John Wooten started out playing right guard for the Browns but was switched to left guard in 1963. He played for them from 1959 to 1967. He was a key component to the team's offensive line when the Browns won the NFL championship over Baltimore in 1964 and when they lost in the title game to Green Bay in 1965. He was a Pro Bowler in 1965 and 1966.

Playing mostly left guard and right guard for Cleveland from 1967 to 1975, John Demarie was a crucial part of talented Browns offensive lines that helped the team to the 1968 and 1969 NFL championship games.

Joe DeLamielleure was a right guard for Cleveland from 1980 to 1984. Although his best days were spent in Buffalo beforehand helping pave the way for O. J. Simpson, DeLamielleure was still a very good player for the Browns. His only Pro Bowl season with the team was in 1980. He was enshrined in the Pro Football Hall of Fame in 2003.

Dan Fike was a stalwart at right guard for the Browns from 1985 to 1989, a period when the team qualified for the postseason all five years and came within one win of the Super Bowl three times. Fike wound down his Browns days as a right tackle his last three seasons through 1992.

Joel Bitonio has been a key cog to the Browns' offensive line at left guard since 2014. He played on some pretty awful Browns teams early in his career, but now that they are winning more, he is getting much deserved recognition. He has been a Pro Bowler every season since 2018.

The players in contention for best Browns guards ever are Houston, Smith, Hickerson, and Wooten.

Joel Bitonio signing an autograph during training camp in 2016
(TRACY EVANS/DREAMSTIME.COM)

LIN HOUSTON

Lin Houston was, hands down, one of the best guards in Browns history.

"You ask Jim Houston, Lin's brother, how good Lin was and he'd tell you how great a player he was," said Steve King. "He was a starter on all those great Browns teams of the 1940s and '50s. He was a great player. Because he was on great teams with great teammates, he never got his due. Offensive line play was big to Paul Brown, and Houston being a starter for all of those seasons with all of those great teams says something about how good he was."

"He was a very good player," said Dan Coughlin.

JIM RAY SMITH

When the subject is greatest offensive linemen in Browns history, the name Jim Ray Smith does not come up very often.

"Smith was a guy who slipped through the cracks," said Steve King. "Because he was one of those players who played in the late '50s and kind of transcended into the '60s, he was part of both eras with Gene Hickerson and Lou Groza, all those guys. He was every bit as good as those guys. He was a great player, but because of when he played he kind of got lost in the shuffle. He was borderline a Hall of Fame lineman. I asked him one time, 'Do you think you were as good as Hickerson and all of those other linemen?' Very sheepishly, he said, 'Yes.'"

"Smith was a great player," said Bob Dolgan. "He was the guard who could pull out and lead the way for Jim Brown."

"Jim Ray was probably the best guard who I have been around in my day," John Wooten said. "He was just an outstanding player."

GENE HICKERSON

Two years before he made his NFL debut with the Browns, Gene Hickerson was paid a compliment by one of his teammates at the University of Mississippi.

"In the summer of 1956, I met Gene Hickerson for the first time," said Robert Khayat, a teammate of Hickerson that year and the next, on OleMissSports.com soon after his death. "He was the finest physical specimen I had seen and he had remarkable speed."

That remarkable speed was one major reason that Hickerson excelled at the NFL level. "To me, Hickerson was one of the greatest offensive linemen ever ... a sprinter!" declared Mike Peticca. "Look at all those game films in which it almost looks like Jim Brown, and later Leroy Kelly, are trying to catch up with him on that sweep! I just remember Hickerson taking care of one guy around the line of scrimmage or just beyond it, then running out and taking care of another would-be tackler.

How many offensive linemen are fun to watch? Not many, but he was. What an amazing player."

"Gene was a tremendous player, he really was," Fred Hoaglin recalled. "I was in awe of the things that I got to see him do. I don't know if he was really recognized as much as he should've been because I can't think of anybody who played then who could do his job better than him. He could still run a 4.7, 4.8 [in the 40-yard dash]. He was the fastest lineman on our team. I went to his Hall of Fame induction, and they show a highlight film of the players when they're inducted. When they showed Gene pulling and running out in front of Leroy Kelly, and Leroy holding on to his jersey so he could keep up with him . . . the fans got to oohing and ahhing pretty loud because they probably hadn't seen that before."

"Gene Hickerson was one of the great pulling guards," said Paul Warfield. "His credentials speak for themselves. He was a great, great offensive lineman. In those years, what you saw from offensive linemen, and particularly what you don't see today . . . the run is not featured in pro football as much today as it was in previous years to some degree. Your offensive linemen back then had to be mobile. In other words, they had to be able not only to block straight ahead in pass protection but certainly in the Browns' offensive fundamentals in running football . . . two to three offensive linemen would pull from their positions and swing laterally right or left on running plays. Gene Hickerson was the master at doing that. He had great mobility as well as outstanding speed to get ahead of runners like Leroy Kelly, Jim Brown, and Ernie Green. He was very versatile, very athletic, very powerful."

"He just personified power, and he could run. He was big and fast," said Tom Melody.

"They talk about guys like Jerry Kramer and Larry Little," Jim Ninowski, a Browns quarterback in 1958 and 1959 and from 1962 to 1966, said, "but Gene was as good, if not better, than all of those guys."

JOHN WOOTEN

Had he played for another team, John Wooten might have gone to more Pro Bowls than he did.

"Because the Browns had so many guys going to the Pro Bowl and being named All-Pro, Wooten was a little overlooked. He was an athletic player, a very good player," said Steve King. "Of the Browns' linemen at the time, he was probably the most athletic they had. You want to have great players at all five positions on the line, but if you can be strong inside with two guards and a center, you can avoid a lot of problems because you don't allow penetration up the middle, you're able to run plays, you're able to get running plays started. And Wooten was that guy."

Wooten was an outstanding player. He was a little bit unsung. In the era in which he played, the mobility of the offensive linemen was unbelievable. "You just don't see that anymore," Paul Warfield said. "John was a great team leader and very instrumental to the great success that Jim Brown had as well as Leroy Kelly. We had two of the best guards. They always talk about the Green Bay guards who were outstanding in that era, too. But certainly our two in John Wooten and Gene Hickerson were equal to those guys."

"When John Morrow got hurt and I had to play the next week," said Fred Hoaglin, "John Wooten helped me to stay levelheaded and think about what was important on each play that we'd be able to do. He was also a highly qualified player."

"I had a pretty good career," said Wooten. "I was pretty happy with the way I moved."

AND THE WINNERS ARE . . .

Gene Hickerson takes one of the slots as best Browns guards ever. He was a multiple First-Team All-Pro and a multiple Pro Bowler. There were other seasons in which he would have been more than deserving of those honors.

The other slot for best Browns guards ever goes to **Jim Ray Smith**. Like Hickerson, Smith was a First-Team All-Pro several times and a Pro Bowler many times.

GUARDS WHO DID NOT MAKE THE CUT

Abe Gibron was an exceptional player who played when the Browns had loads of exceptional players.

"Gibron was a great guard, but because he played with all those great players, he kind of got lost in the shuffle," said Steve King.

"He was one of the Browns' best guards," Bob Dolgan said. "The Browns were known as a finesse team in the 1940s and '50s, a lot of passing, but they had a lot of tough characters who could really take care of themselves, and Gibron was one of them."

John Demarie gave 100 percent all the time.

"John was a good player, tough and hardnosed," said Fred Hoaglin. "He was intense, too, played hard."

"Demarie was a very good player who stepped in and kind of got the Browns through that transitional era coming out of the '60s into the '70s," said King. "He was solid."

Joe DeLamielleure had no training camp in his first season with the Browns because he was traded to them from Buffalo less than a week before the season opener.

"I played a little bit in the first game, and after that I played all the time. It was an adjustment," he said. "You get used to the guys. Tom DeLeone and Cody Risien were the two guys I really worked with, the center, DeLeone, and Risien, the right tackle. We adapted quickly to each other, and we had a good year."

DeLamielleure came to Cleveland with a great reputation, especially renowned because of blocking for O. J. Simpson. And everybody could see why he *had* that reputation. "The way that he could pull and block downfield, his speed, his pass-blocking," said Mike Peticca. "That really anchored the offensive line when they got him. He definitely merits his Hall of Fame status. He was a great player and was still in his prime the first three years the Browns had him. What a bonus that was."

"The Browns needed Joe DeLamielleure at that time," King said. "The 1980 Browns wanted to go for broke, they wanted to try to win a championship, and if you get a chance to get a Hall of Fame player like Joe DeLamielleure, you do that. He wasn't the player he was when he was with the 'Electric Company' in Buffalo, but he was a very good player. If you look at what he did during that 1980 season, that really helped fortify the middle of that line. Some of the players in 1980 didn't like Henry Sheppard and Robert [E.] Jackson losing playing time to DeLamielleure, but Sam Rutigliano's retort to that was, 'Hey, if you get a chance to get a Hall of Famer, you bring him in.'"

"DeLamielleure was just a worker, and he took pride in that," said Jeff Schudel. "He was a very good run blocker. He was a bulldozer."

Versatility was a huge reason for **Dan Fike**'s success at the NFL level during the late 1980s and early 1990s. He was one of the most versatile players the Browns had at the time. "He could play either guard spot, center, or tackle. He could do everything," said King. "He was kind of the quiet, laid back Texan, and whatever the Browns asked him to do, he'd do it. Wherever he played, he played very well. He was a good player."

"Fike was versatile and he was big," Peticca said. "You could see him use that length. He was probably quicker than you would've envisioned. I think he was an excellent athlete. I can still picture him getting out in front of guys. He utilized those physical gifts he had to be a fine pass blocker. He had to be tough to get past, get around, get over. I think he's really underrated as you look back to those teams."

"Dan was a bellringer for the offensive line during the Marty Schottenheimer years," Ray Yannucci said. "He was a heck of a player, a big guy."

"He would play hurt," said Jeff Schudel. "His knees were bad, but he never let it show."

Joel Bitonio is a player who reminds people of yesteryear. He is a throwback player. He has that toughness, that snarly, deep-down-in-the-dirt attitude.

"Joel kind of reminds me of an old-school guard," said Doug Dieken. "He's tough, he's smart, he's a good player. He's just one of those guys who every Sunday . . . he has that dependability and consistency that you always look for."

"He's a very good lineman," King said. "Now that the Browns have better linemen around him, guess what? He's gotten better. He could've played in any era."

"Joel is a lot like Joe Thomas in that he's an athletic guard, and he's a big guy," said Schudel. "He's obviously improved a lot over the years. He's got a great attitude, and he's unselfish. He's a big part of the offensive line."

"That was one of the better draft picks the Browns had before the present regime came in," added Mike McLain. "It's surprising they hit on one because they were missing on everybody. His first couple years, he was getting dinged a lot, but he's become a very good offensive lineman. He's kind of the linchpin to that group."

CENTER

THE CANDIDATES

Frank Gatski
John Morrow
Alex Mack

Frank Gatski doesn't get the headlines when the subject is Browns Hall of Famers, but he should because he was as rock solid as one could be as a center for Cleveland from 1946 to 1956. The 1985 Hall of Fame inductee created big holes for Marion Motley, Edgar Jones, and Dub Jones. He helped protect Otto Graham en route to 10 championship-game appearances, seven of them triumphs. Gatski was First-Team All-Pro in 1952, 1953, and 1955 and a Pro Bowler in 1956.

John Morrow played center for the Browns from 1960 to 1966. He was one of the best centers in team history. He blocked for Jim Brown and Bobby Mitchell and helped protect Frank Ryan. He was the Browns' starting center in the 1964 NFL championship-game victory over the Colts. He was a Pro Bowler in 1961 and 1963.

Taking over at center for Morrow was Fred Hoaglin, who manned the position from 1966 to 1972. He blocked for Leroy Kelly and Ernie Green and protected Ryan and Bill Nelsen. He was picked for the Pro Bowl in 1969.

Tom DeLeone played center for Cleveland from 1974 to 1984. He wasn't the biggest at his position, but he had all the moves and the quickness to be one of the best centers in team history. He was a Pro Bowler in 1979 and 1980.

Replacing DeLeone at the center position was Mike Baab. Baab had two stints with the Browns—from 1982 to 1987 and in 1990 and 1991. He was never a Pro Bowler, but he was as dependable as any player could be, playing in nearly every game from his second season on.

Alex Mack was one of the few draft picks by the expansion Browns that actually worked out well. A first-round draft pick in 2009, he shined for the Browns for seven seasons, from 2009 to 2015. He was a Pro Bowler in 2010, 2013, and 2015.

The three players who are in the running for best Browns center of all time are Gatski, Morrow, and Mack.

FRANK GATSKI

There was nothing grandiose about Frank Gatski.

"He was one of the toughest, most unique guys the Browns have ever had," said Steve King. "There was nothing pretentious about this guy. He grew up in a tiny, little burg in West Virginia, and the little town never got out of him. He didn't want any pomp with anything, he just wanted to play football and wanted to keep things simple. It's been said that you build a team up the middle. Well, the last piece of that for the Browns of the 1940s and '50s was Frank Gatski."

"Frank was just an old pro," said Jim Ray Smith. "He was a good center. He just kind of fit in there at center."

"He was a hardnosed player," Ray Yannucci said. "He looked like he was really, really a tough guy in the Chuck Bednarik mold, and he was."

Gatski was the first Browns lineman who was a weightlifter. He was way ahead of his time. "Nobody else lifted weights back then," said Dan Coughlin. "He was considered the best center in the NFL during the peak of his career."

"He was a heck of a player, a very strong player, a tough guy," Bob Dolgan said.

JOHN MORROW

The one player people seem to forget on the great Browns' offensive lines in the 1960s is John Morrow.

"Morrow was as solid of a center as there was in the league," said Steve King. "Maybe he wasn't Mick Tingelhoff, maybe he wasn't a Hall of Famer, but he was solid. You very seldom saw the middle of the line crumble or saw somebody miss a block, and that was in large part due to John Morrow. He was a smart guy. Without him, the Browns would not have won the championship in 1964. He played a great, great game in that championship game against Baltimore."

"I had great respect for John Morrow," Paul Warfield said. "He was a very smart guy, and you always want a very heady individual to play center because he has to call the blocking for those individuals who are to his left and to his right. And he was very adept at doing that. He was very tough and a great competitor."

Very rarely was there ever a bad snap from Morrow. "I just remember him as coming off the ball really quick after the snap and taking on those big interior linemen very well," said Mike Peticca.

"John was a hardworking guy, a tough, never-give-up type of player," said John Wooten. "He got every ounce of his ability in his play."

"I learned a lot from John," Fred Hoaglin said.

ALEX MACK

Because Alex Mack attended the University of California, Berkeley, it is no surprise that he is an intelligent guy.

"Alex is a real smart guy," said Doug Dieken. "The thing about Alex was if there was a running play, you'd see him 10–15 yards down the field every time. Besides being smart and strong, he hustled his ass off."

"I remember the Browns trading down in 2009 when they drafted Mack. That proved to be a really good pick when you see what he did for them," Jeff Schudel said. "He was so smart. He recognized what the defense was doing, and he'd get the signals to his line mates."

Mack was one of the better centers in team history. He was just a beast of a man. His ability to get downfield to that second level was pretty much unmatched by a lot of centers who have played for the Browns. "You talk about great centers, there's Alex Mack. He was a solid player," said Steve King. "He was worth every bit of his draft positioning. He was tired of losing and years spent on a team that was below mediocrity. It was sad that he left [via free agency]."

AND THE WINNER IS . . .

Frank Gatski is unmatched in Browns history as far as the best center ever. He was durable, he was tough, and he played on championship teams. He was a big part of the Browns' success in their early years.

John Morrow may not be the first player mentioned when the subject is greatest Browns players of all time, but talk to his opponents, talk to opposing nose guards and linebackers, and see what they say. Morrow was as good as they come.

It is too bad that Alex Mack didn't stick around with the Browns longer than he did. It would have been nice to see him experience the success the team is now enjoying. He was simply tired of playing for a losing organization, and that is why he left the Browns after the 2015 season. In his very first season with Atlanta, he did get to start on the Falcons team that played in Super Bowl LI.

Frank Gatski gets the nod as the Browns' all-time best center.

CENTERS WHO DID NOT MAKE THE CUT

Fred Hoaglin was a solid center for the Browns for several years, but he does not exactly get bells and whistles when the topic is greatest Browns linemen of all time.

"He was an unsung player," said Steve King. "He was a great player."

"When I got to Cleveland, Freddy was one of the leaders on the offensive line," said Doug Dieken.

"I had a lot of fun playing for the Browns," said Hoaglin. "I enjoyed it."

Tom DeLeone was a scrappy player and a good player, too.

"Tom was one of the feistiest guys in the world," said Dieken. "If the other team wanted to fight, he'd be the first in line. He wasn't the biggest guy in the world, but he was probably one of the quickest centers who I've ever seen. He learned that if he could get in position, the guy wouldn't run him over."

"He was a tough guy, hardnosed," Joe DeLamielleure said. "He was the leader on the offensive line, which most centers are. He'd do whatever he had to do to block. He wasn't a big guy, but he was quick, unbelievably quick. That's how he played. When the opponent played a 4-3 defense, he was a nightmare for the middle linebacker."

"If I wanted to walk into a dark alley, I wanted Tom DeLeone next to me," said Ray Yannucci. "That's how tough he was."

"He was undersized but was still very good at keeping people off the quarterback. He held his own," said Mike Pruitt.

In the 1980 Kardiac Kids season, Brian Sipe was sacked only 23 times. "DeLeone was in the middle of that, making the blocking calls and making sure nobody came clean," King said. "He was just a great player."

"Fred and Tom were very good centers and outstanding players in their own right," said Paul Warfield. "I had a great appreciation for their efforts and preparation and also for the abilities in which they provided excellent protection in the passing game and also the ability to enhance the running game with their blocking."

When DeLeone hurt his ankle early in the 1983 season, **Mike Baab** took his place. "Whereas Tom's game was quickness, Mike's was strength. He was a powerful guy," said Dieken. "The guys accepted him, and he was a good player for a long time."

"Mike turned out to be a very good center," said Pruitt.

Baab came in and, as the Browns reassembled themselves through the last half of the 1980s, just took over. In the 1987 AFC Championship Game he got hurt and did not play the second half. The Browns had drafted Gregg Rakoczy, and he played very well in Baab's spot the rest of the game, but Baab's absence made a difference and showed his importance to the team. The Browns wound up trading Baab because they didn't feel they needed him. "Bernie Kosar came into the offensive meeting room that day, and when he found out the Browns had let Baab go, he slammed his playbook on the desk," King recalled. "Well, the first game of the 1988 season at Kansas City, there was a blitz and Kosar got blindsided and injured his arm. And, all of a sudden, the season starts to come unglued. That would not have happened had Mike Baab been there. Baab would've made the right call, he would've made sure everybody was on the same page. He was a smart player, a cerebral player, a very good player. The Browns blew it on that one."

"The thing I remember most is how upset the players were when the Browns traded Baab," said Mike Peticca. "I think that says almost as much as anything else how valuable he was. His attitude, his nature, helped create a toughness that made that line really good. He was obviously technically and fundamentally a very, very good player. Center is where it all starts, and I think he inspired confidence in the quarterback and across the rest of the line. He was a very smart player, too."

"He was a good football player," Mike McLain added. "I don't know if he was as mobile as some of the other centers, but he was a part of that group that developed pretty well there in the '80s and brought excitement to Browns fans."

TIGHT END

Milt Morin
Ozzie Newsome

Pete Brewster put up solid numbers for the Browns from 1952 to 1958. His receptions/receiving yards ratios from 1953 to 1957 were, respectively, 32/632, 42/676, 34/622, 28/417, and 30/614. He had six touchdown receptions in 1955 and four in both 1953 and 1954. His 20.5 yards per reception in 1957 led the entire NFL. He was a Pro Bowler in 1955 and 1956.

Johnny Brewer was a tight end for the Browns from 1962 to 1965 before switching to linebacker in 1966. He had some decent numbers as a tight end, his best season coming in 1963 when he caught 29 passes for 454 yards. His lone Pro Bowl year was 1966, his first season as a linebacker.

Milt Morin was a very talented player for the Browns from 1966 to 1975. His two best years were his only Pro Bowl seasons—1968 and 1971. In 1968, he had 43 receptions for 792 yards with five touchdowns. In 1971, he caught 40 passes for 581 yards with two touchdowns. He was a key factor in Cleveland's playoff runs in 1968, 1969, 1971, and 1972.

When it comes to tight ends in Browns history, Ozzie Newsome is the player who most people know of as the best.

His numbers validate it. He played for the Browns from 1978 to 1990. He had two seasons—1981 and 1984—in which he topped 1,000 yards in receiving. He had 89 receptions twice—in 1983 and 1984. He had nine touchdown catches in 1979 and six in both 1981 and 1983. Newsome had great hands and was known for making incredible catches. He was First-Team All-Pro in 1984 and was a Pro Bowler in 1981, 1984, and 1985. He was enshrined into the Pro Football Hall of Fame in 1999.

In the running for best Browns tight end of all time are Morin and Newsome.

MILT MORIN

The tight end position changed with Milt Morin.

"Mainly," said Paul Warfield, "the tight end position when I first joined the Browns was more in the blocking scheme, and the catching scheme was devoted mainly to the wide receivers. Milt Morin turned out to be certainly an excellent blocker. He was a big man. He had great mobility to get off of the line of scrimmage, get into the passing game but yet also could be a very effective blocker. He brought a little bit more catching abilities."

Morin was a big guy with great hands and was really strong. He could get a lot of yards after the catch just by running over or through opponents. He also had some speed. "He had to be one of those guys who the safeties didn't necessarily want to take on with him going full speed," Mike Peticca said. "He was a bull. He approached greatness because he was also an excellent blocker."

"Milt was a great player," said Fred Hoaglin. "He was so big. He was big enough to play tackle at that time. He was really a great pass receiver and a good blocker. And he was awesome running with the ball because he had to be like what a safety might have seen if Jim Brown broke through the line of scrimmage. It had to be that kind of feeling for them to try to tackle Milt because he was big. He was tough. He was one of the first of the real big tight ends."

"Other than Ozzie Newsome, he was the greatest tight end the Browns have ever had," Steve King said. "He caught the ball when it was thrown to him, and he ran over people. He was a viable target. Everyone would be paying attention to [Gary] Collins and Warfield, here comes Milt Morin. He was a guy who could make big plays."

OZZIE NEWSOME
If Milt Morin changed the tight end position, Ozzie Newsome revolutionized it.

"Ozzie was the prototype because he could play tight end, and he threatened the defense just like a wide receiver," Sam Rutigliano said in the February 2005 *Bernie's Insiders*. "When he came into the NFL, what was in vogue at the time was defenses playing what they called 'double zone' where two safeties would each cover half the field. Ozzie drove that defense out of football because of his ability as a tight end to run like a wide receiver and attack the middle of the field."

Newsome was actually a wide receiver in college for the University of Alabama. Throughout the draft process, some teams were saying they would allow him to stay at wide receiver, others were asking him if he would consider a move to tight end. He actually got drafted by Cleveland as a receiver. "I went through my first minicamp as a wide receiver," he said. "It was interesting that the week they had the rookie minicamp I called Sam and said, 'You know, I'd like to not participate in that because that's the week of graduation, and my family wants to see me graduate.' He allowed me to do that. So I went in with the veterans the following week. I was the only rookie who was at the veteran camp. And those three days I worked at wide receiver. They wanted to keep some guys for an additional three or four days, and I was one of them. Sam said to me, 'You know, you could be a good receiver in this league, there's no doubt. You just proved that over the last three days of this minicamp. But we think you could be a *great* tight end. And we're going to move you to tight end with your willingness, but if we're going to move you, we're going to throw you the football. We're going to throw you a lot of footballs at tight end.' He was very honest and very truthful, and that's what they did, and that's how I accepted the move. My personal preference was catching the football . . . because, see, I'd played in a wishbone in college, and so you weren't getting but three or four passes a day, so blocking was not a problem."

"That gave Ozzie an opportunity to block linebackers," said Rutigliano. "We never asked him to block defensive ends, but playing him at tight end opened the door for [receiver] Reggie Rucker, opened the door for [receiver] Dave Logan, opened the door for the running backs, because every game we played, the defense was trying to defend Ozzie."

Newsome was in awe during his first game in the NFL against San Francisco on September 3, 1978. At that point, he was still wondering if he could actually play in the league. "I'd had some success in the preseason but you're still, 'Can you really play?'" he said. "And getting myself prepared . . . there's one thing about what the veterans will tell you. They say, 'Well, you know what? Playing in the preseason is a lot different than playing in the regular season. But, then also, playing in the regular season is a little different than when you play against Pittsburgh. It's three different levels.' So, they had forewarned me that now it's for real. And, then, you know you're standing on the same field that O. J. Simpson is in that 49ers game. And that added to the awe that I was in. You know, 'Hey, I'm getting ready to play against The Juice.' But once the game starts, it's the

Ozzie Newsome taking a breather (JERRY COLI/DREAMSTIME.COM)

game. Football is football. The first time I touched the ball was on the [34-yard] end-around. I scored a touchdown.

"Soon after I got to Cleveland, people would talk to me and would be like, 'Oh, you're the draft choice . . . ya'll gonna beat Pittsburgh this year?' See, we had never beaten them in Three Rivers Stadium. So, you start to realize that, and they were comparing the rivalry to me, 'Well, it's bigger than your Alabama-Auburn rivalry.' And I go, 'What? Bigger than Alabama-Auburn?' And they say, 'Yes. It is.' So, right away, you realize the importance of it, but, at that time, Pittsburgh . . . they had already won two Super Bowls, and you just start to think about the players who they had playing. So, again, this is me being on the field with a bunch of future Hall of Famers that I grew up idolizing . . . Stallworth, Swann and Franco and Joe Greene and Mel Blount, and now I'm on the same field with those guys."

"I remember watching Newsome in his last college game against Ohio State in the Sugar Bowl and I'm thinking, 'Man, that guy is good,' Mike McLain recalled. "Clearly, he was a great route runner and had great hands. He was part of that revival of the tight end with Dave Casper and Kellen Winslow, Jr. They redefined that position. Newsome was a true Hall of Famer on and off the field."

"Four weeks into my rookie season we signed Calvin Hill," recalled Newsome. "He kind of took me under his wing. He was somebody who I'd respected growing up, and to spend time with someone like that was invaluable."

"What can you say about Ozzie? The 'Wiz'," said Mike Pruitt. "You threw him the ball, and I don't care if it was eight feet high, he'd come down with it. He just had great hands. Anything you'd throw anywhere close to him, he'd catch it! He always got open, and he always caught the ball. That's why he's in the Hall of Fame."

Said Rutigliano in reverence, "Ozzie dropped one pass in the six-and-a-half years I was with him."

AND THE WINNER IS . . .

Milt Morin was a fabulous tight end for 10 seasons with the Browns. He was not only big, but he was fast. He could run through defenders or around them. He was a very important piece of the puzzle that resulted in five trips to the postseason.

Ozzie Newsome? Well, there is really not much that can be said about him than what fans already know. For 13 seasons, he was a Hall of Fame tight end. He had some great seasons when the Browns did not fare too well, but he was also a cornerstone of the playoff teams in the late 1980s. It will be a long time before the Browns find another Ozzie Newsome.

It should come as no surprise then that **Ozzie Newsome** is our choice for the greatest tight end in Browns history.

TIGHT ENDS WHO DID NOT MAKE THE CUT

Pete Brewster was a solid tight end.

"He was a pretty good player, a pretty good receiver," said Steve King. "He made catches and played well. He was the leading receiver or second in receiving during some of those seasons."

"Pete was a good ballplayer. He ran good routes," said Jim Ray Smith.

The Browns' coaching staff did not care if **Johnny Brewer** caught a single ball. "All they cared about was how good of a blocker I was," Brewer said.

There are those who claim that Brewer was the greatest blocking tight end in the NFL at the time. "Our offense was one of the finest around with Jim Brown and Ernie Green in the backfield," he said. "We ran the strong-side sweep a lot, and the key block on that play is the tight end's because the pulling guard doesn't get out in front of the ball carrier."

The Browns utilized Brewer, and their emphasis was running and utilization of a tight end more in the blocking scheme than the receiving scheme. "John was absolutely the best," said Paul Warfield. "He could control the linebacker playing on the end. He was vital to the running attack and proved to be a great, great blocking tight end."

"We thought we had a sixth lineman in Brewer," said Dick Schafrath. "He could catch the ball, but he was who made Jim Brown, Leroy Kelly, and Ernie Green run because he could take that outside linebacker."

Brewer, though, was capable of making clutch catches at times. "Johnny didn't have the facility of catching the ball as well as some of our other pass catchers," Frank Ryan recalled, "but he was very good when there was a real need to have him make a play."

WIDE RECEIVERS

The Candidates

Dante Lavelli
Mac Speedie
Ray Renfro
Gary Collins
Paul Warfield

Dante Lavelli never had a thousand-yard receiving season, but it didn't matter. He still had the stats that were more than good enough to warrant his induction into the Pro Football Hall of Fame in 1975. Right from his rookie season with the Browns in 1946 through 1956, he was "Mr. Clutch." With the Browns trailing the New York Yankees, 9–7, in the fourth quarter of the 1946 AAFC championship game, Lavelli caught a 16-yard touchdown pass from Otto Graham for what turned out to be the winning score in a 14–9 Browns triumph. That season, Lavelli led the AAFC with 40 receptions, 843 receiving yards, and 21.1 yards per reception. He also had eight touchdown catches. In a time when teams didn't pass the ball nearly as much as they do today, Lavelli had 49 receptions for 799 yards with nine touchdowns in 1947 and 43 catches for 586 yards with six touchdowns in 1951. In 1953, he had 45 receptions for 783 yards with six touchdowns, and the next year, he caught 47 passes for 802 yards with seven touchdowns. He was a member of Browns teams that appeared in 10 straight championship games in his first 10 seasons. He was a Pro Bowler in 1951, 1953, and 1954.

Mac Speedie always seemed to play second fiddle to Lavelli, but Speedie was a great receiver in his own right. In fact, he had two thousand-yard receiving seasons and nearly had a third. He had 67 receptions for 1,146 yards with six touchdowns, including a team-record 99-yarder, in 1947. The next season, he caught 58 passes for 816 yards with four touchdowns. In 1949, he had 62 receptions for 1,028 yards with seven touchdowns, and in his last season in 1952 he caught 62 passes for 911 yards with five touchdowns. He was First-Team All-Pro from 1947 to 1949 and was picked for the Pro Bowl in 1950 and 1952. Had he not left the NFL for the Canadian Football League in 1953, Speedie very well may have been a Hall of Famer.

In Ray Renfro's dozen seasons with the Browns from 1952 to 1963, he put up some pretty gaudy numbers. He had 281 career receptions for 5,508 yards with 50 touchdowns. His most impressive stat, however, was his career 19.6 yards per reception. Five times, he eclipsed 20 yards per reception with 28 yards per catch in 1957 leading the way. He was very consistent throughout his career. He was a Pro Bowler in 1953, 1957, and 1960.

Gary Collins always seemed to make a big catch when the Browns needed one in his career with the team that lasted from 1962 to 1971. Like Lavelli, he never had a thousand-yard receiving season, but he was a clutch receiver. In Cleveland's four NFL championship-game appearances from 1964 to 1969, he scored all five of the Browns' touchdowns, including three in the team's 27–0 whitewashing of heavily favored Baltimore in 1964. His best season came in 1966 when he had 56 receptions for 946 yards with 12 touchdowns. The season before, he caught 50 passes for 884 yards with 10 touchdowns. His 13 touchdown receptions in 1963 led the NFL. Collins was a Pro Bowler in 1965 and 1966.

Paul Warfield was as graceful as they come when it comes to wide receivers. He was smooth and looked like he was gliding when running with the ball after a catch. He made it look so easy during his two stints with the Browns from 1964 to 1969 and in 1976 and 1977. He may not have had the most receptions in the NFL, but when he caught a pass it was usually a long gainer. He averaged 19.2 yards per catch in his eight seasons with Cleveland. His three best seasons with the Browns were 1964, 1968, and 1969, not coincidentally three years in which the Browns played in the NFL championship game, the first of which they won. And, also not coincidentally, those were his only Pro Bowl years with the Browns. In 1964, Warfield's rookie season, he had 52 receptions for 920 yards with nine touchdowns. In 1968, he caught 50 passes for 1,067 yards with a league-leading 12 touchdowns. The next season, he had 42 receptions for 886 yards with 10 touchdowns. He was inducted into the Pro Football Hall of Fame in 1983.

In his seven seasons with the Browns from 1975 to 1981, Reggie Rucker, although not a true burner, found a way to get open and made a lot of catches. In his very first season with Cleveland, he led the AFC with 60 receptions. His receptions/receiving yardage ratios from 1978 to 1980, respectively, were 43/893, 43/749, and 52/768. He had eight touchdown catches in both 1976 and 1978.

Dave Logan had the best pair of hands of perhaps any Browns wide receiver ever. He made some one-handed catches that were simply spectacular. Maybe the best one came in a 1979 game against the Pittsburgh Steelers when he reached with his left hand in front of Donnie Shell and caught a ball thrown by Brian Sipe for a touchdown. A photo of that play appeared on the cover of the following season's *Sports Illustrated* pro football preview issue. Logan's two best seasons not surprisingly came in the Kardiac Kids years of 1979 and 1980. In 1979, he had 59 receptions for 982 yards with seven touchdowns, and in 1980 he caught 51 passes for 822 yards with four touchdowns.

Brian Brennan had a knack for getting open. He wasn't big, he wasn't fast, but oh boy, could he ever get open. And he had great hands. In his eight seasons with Cleveland from 1984 to 1991, he totaled 315 receptions for 4,148 yards with 19 touchdowns. His best season was in 1986 when he had 55 receptions for 838 yards with six touchdowns. In the AFC title game against Denver that year, right before The Drive, Brennan caught a 48-yard touchdown pass from Bernie Kosar to give the Browns a 20–13 lead late in the game. That catch also had nearly 80,000 fans in attendance believing that the Browns were on their way to Super Bowl XXI.

Reggie Langhorne was a seventh-round draft choice of the Browns in 1985 out of tiny Elizabeth City State University in North Carolina. Not much was expected of him. He was a longshot to even make the team. But make the team he did, and in 1986 it began paying dividends. That year, he had 39 receptions for 678 yards with a touchdown; that TD was a big one, a 55-yarder from Kosar that gave the Browns a fourth-quarter lead they would not relinquish in a Week 2 win in Houston that kept the team from falling to 0-2. Langhorne's two best seasons with Cleveland came in 1988 and 1989. In 1988, he had 57 receptions for 780 yards with seven touchdowns, and in 1989 he caught 60 passes for 749 yards with two touchdowns.

Very few Browns fans knew who Webster Slaughter was when he was chosen by the Browns in the second round of the 1986 NFL Draft out of San Diego State University. It didn't take long for fans to realize Slaughter was a talented wide receiver. In his rookie season of 1986, he had 40 receptions for 577 yards with four touchdowns, including a memorable

36-yarder from Kosar in overtime that beat the Steelers 37–31 in a crucial late-season game. Slaughter's three best seasons with Cleveland came from 1989 to 1991 when his receptions/ receiving yards ratios were, respectively, 65/1,236, 59/847, and 64/906. He had seven touchdown catches in 1987 and six in 1989. He caught a 97-yard TD pass from Kosar on October 23, 1989, that helped his team to a 27–7 victory over the Bears on *Monday Night Football*. Slaughter was a Pro Bowler in 1989.

Jarvis Landry has been a Brown for only four seasons, but he has shown enough to be considered one of the top receivers in team history. If he stays healthy, he will be a Hall of Famer, including what he accomplished in four seasons with Miami. In his first season with Cleveland in 2018, he had 81 receptions for 976 yards with four touchdowns. The next year, he caught 83 passes for 1,174 yards with six touchdowns. In 2020, he had 72 receptions for 840 yards with three TDs. He was a Pro Bowler in 2018 and 2019.

Jarvis Landry in action against the Bills in a preseason game on August 17, 2018 (ERIK DROST/WIKIMEDIA COMMONS)

Those in the running for best Browns receivers of all time are Lavelli, Speedie, Renfro, Collins, and Warfield.

DANTE LAVELLI

Dante Lavelli was the main man who Otto Graham searched for when a big catch was needed.

"Anytime Otto got in trouble, Lavelli was the guy he looked to," said Steve King. "They had a tremendous rapport. They called Dante 'Glue Fingers' because he didn't drop many passes. If the ball was near him, he was going to catch it, and if he got his hands on it he caught it."

No one understood what it meant to be a member of those great Browns teams of the early years more than Lavelli. He was proud of what those teams did. "When everybody was making a big deal out of the Miami Dolphins in 1972 going undefeated, Lavelli stood up and said, 'Hey, we were undefeated in 1948,'" King said. "And when everybody was making a big deal about the New England Patriots in 2007 going undefeated until the Super Bowl, Lavelli was on a national interview and said, 'Hey, we were undefeated in 1948.' You couldn't move him off that. As he got older, he got prouder."

"Dante was a great, fun-loving guy, but on the football field he was a tough character," Bob Dolgan said.

"He was one of the all-time greats," added Dan Coughlin.

MAC SPEEDIE

Mac Speedie's overall numbers were actually better than Dante Lavelli's.

"The fact that he didn't get his due was simply because he jumped to the CFL," said Steve King. "He didn't have the nickname like 'Glue Fingers' and didn't have all the charisma of Lavelli, but he was every bit the receiver that Lavelli was. He was just a great player."

"Mac was one of the best players of his time," Ray Yannucci said.

"Every team, I think when you look at them—the 49ers with Rice and Taylor, the Steelers with Stallworth and Swann—has a great set of receivers," said King. "The Browns of the '60s with Warfield and Collins and the Browns of the late '80s with Slaughter, Langhorne, and Brennan. If you look at two Hall of Fame players, there weren't a pair better than Lavelli and Speedie."

RAY RENFRO

One Browns receiver who seems to get overlooked when the subject is great receivers in team annals is Ray Renfro.

"We talk about players on the Browns who don't get their due, and you can't say that more about anyone than you can about Ray Renfro," said Steve King. "He came in at the tail end of the late '40s-early '50s era and played into the early '60s. He was a tremendous player, a great player, but he wasn't Jim Brown, he wasn't Lavelli, he wasn't Speedie. He was a great player, though. If you look at his statistics, every year he had good stats. His average yards per catch was incredible. He was a versatile player. He could do a lot of different things. You could win with him. If you think back to the great players in Browns history, not a lot of people are going to say, 'Ray Renfro.' But there's no question about it, he was a great player."

Renfro was the guy who became the true archetype of the flanker. Said Dan Coughlin, "That's when the game went to three wide receivers and two running backs."

"There's no better route runner who ever came into this league than Ray Renfro," John Wooten said.

"Ray was one of the great receivers in Browns history," added Jim Ray Smith.

GARY COLLINS

Gary Collins was a forerunner to the physically big receivers of today. When teams can find a big man who has the ability and intricacies to do what a great receiver does, he is very special. Collins was unique because of his stature and his body mass. But he was also a very precise pass-catcher who had excellent quickness and very quick feet, and could accelerate in and out of breaks. He also had great hands. He could pluck the ball right out of the air. "And, to my mind, and I've said it over and over," said Paul Warfield, "I've never seen, and certainly during the time that I played in the NFL and perhaps previous to that and even to this day, a receiver who had the ability to be so productive in the red zone. He was unstoppable there. He beat some of the very best defensive backs who are Hall of Famers consistently, year in and year out."

"Gary was a big target, and he had quickness out of his break," said Bill Nelsen, who played quarterback for the Browns from 1968 to 1972. "He didn't necessarily have the great speed, but when he made a cut he did it real fast."

"He was big, he made the tough catches, he hardly dropped a pass, he just kind of projected toughness the way he carried himself," Mike Peticca said. "He made a lot of plays down-field. He was much more than just a possession receiver. If he'd been healthy another couple of years or so, it would've really enhanced his Hall of Fame chances."

Dan Coughlin took it a step further.

"Gary absolutely should be in the Hall of Fame," he said.

Doug Dieken agreed.

"Gary was my hero while I was growing up. He's the guy I wanted to be," he said. "I eventually got a chance to be his team-mate for one season. That was special. Gary is a guy who should be in the Hall of Fame. He was a great receiver."

"If you're a wide receiver," said Collins, "I think the greatest asset you should have is to be able to catch. A lot of today's wide receivers don't think that way. It's, 'I run a 4.4 [in the 40-yard dash].' That's what they think. A lot of these guys, they have no moves. They run that go-pattern and out-jump a guy."

For all of his greatness, Collins will forever be known for the 1964 championship-game upset win over the Colts in which he caught three touchdown passes from Frank Ryan. The brash Collins was doing interviews with the media before the game. "You're 24 years old," he recalled, "and a guy puts a mike in front of you and says, 'Well Gary, you're seven-point underdogs. You think you're gonna win the game?' What am I gonna say, 'We're going to lose?' So I come out and I said, while sitting there in the old locker room at League Park, our practice site, 'We're going to win big. I'm not even worried about it.' And people are laughing. They were calling me 'Cocky kid.' But that's the way I felt. That's the way I played football—with confidence."

As for the game itself, it was the Browns' defense and the Ryan-to-Collins hookups that ruled the day. "Gary and I had started developing a connection back in '62," said Ryan, "when he was a 'freshman' and I was in my first year with the Browns. We'd work after practice with Blanton Collier, who was an offensive assistant coach then, working on moves and anticipating things and what not, me anticipating where he was going and him understanding when the ball would be there and all that sort of stuff. Gary was a fine person and a very fine football player. He gave you a lot of confidence throwing the ball, and he sure let you know if you didn't throw it right. He was outspoken, but he was always right. He never did anything in a petty way. And he desperately wanted to win. He was a winner."

"The Colts' strategy," Warfield recalled, "was problematic for me because they set their defenses in particular passing situations to take me out of the ballgame with forms of double

Gary Collins attempting to catch the ball against the Cardinals in the late 1960s (PAUL TEPLEY/CLEVELAND STATE UNIVERSITY CLEVELAND PRESS ARCHIVES)

coverage. In doing that, they were going to be at risk as far as Gary was concerned simply because he was so good that you couldn't cover him man-for-man either. Gary, with his great size, great hands, and great maneuverability, just overwhelmed Bobby Boyd and was truly unstoppable. And that was kind of the makeup of our offense during those years. You had to pick your poison."

Collins dislikes the egomaniacal nature of many of today's professional athletes.

"All you do is you shoot baskets, or you hit a baseball, or you catch a football, or you throw a football," he said. "You don't do anything like develop a vaccine. Do something important before thinking you're important."

Paul Warfield

Because of his growing reputation on the defensive side of the ball, Paul Warfield was actually drafted by the Browns as a cornerback. But, because he played a little at wide receiver while at Ohio State University, the Browns took a passing look at him as a receiver. It was at the one-day rookie minicamp at Lakewood High School in the late spring of 1964 that Blanton Collier made the decision that Warfield was not going to be a cornerback, that he was going to be a wide receiver.

"I found out when I got to training camp at Hiram," he recalled. "I was elated!"

Warfield would get the chance to work with an accomplished veteran receiver who had a great career in Ray Renfro, his personal mentor for the first month of training camp his rookie season. "Ray was going to pass on all of his knowledge to me about pass receiving," he said. "He was one of the first speed guys in that era. He was a 9.5 100-yard sprinter. The Cleveland Browns were a team that, and Paul Brown had been a coach who, enjoyed throwing the football. The Browns had one of the most sophisticated systems for throwing the football far in advance, even when they were in the old AAFC. They were far ahead of anyone else in terms of pass receiving and throwing

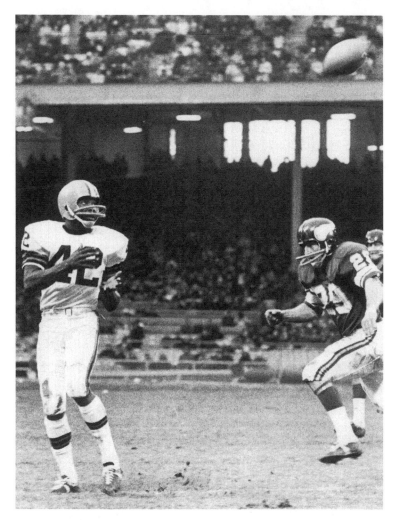

Paul Warfield in action early in his career (PAUL TEPLEY/CLEVELAND STATE UNIVERSITY CLEVELAND PRESS ARCHIVES)

the football. So I was going to get a chance to learn from an individual who'd been a part of this magnificent system.

"The things that Ray Renfro taught me over that four-week period contributed to my being able to make the transition to the pros and have some immediate success in the National Football League. Furthermore, the things he taught me fundamentally in terms of execution I never deviated from, from day one to the final day of my football career. As I gained more experience, of course, I added a few things here and there, but the basic foundation of my game in terms of pass receiving, getting open, and catching the football was formed in those four weeks. In addition, Ray gave me insights into the game that I'd never even thought of, like how to set up defenders, how to execute in certain situations, and how to get into the end zone. I had great physical talent to play football, but I had never been invited to look at it from a cerebral, or mental, side of it, and he opened up that door for me."

Focus and concentration in pass receiving were priorities for Warfield.

"When the ball was in the air," he said, "the first thing I tried to do was make sure, that when I made my break one direction or another, my head turned back instantaneously at the time of making a break because I wanted to find and locate the football as quickly as possible. I wanted to see it almost coming off the fingertips of the passer and then follow it all the way in flight into my hands.

"The desire to catch the football must be will and competitiveness, that when the ball is in the air, it belongs to no one except me, and I'm going after it. There are going to be other people in the area, but I don't see or feel them. I see the ball in the air, and I'm going to go after it with all the zest that I have. I credit Ray Renfro for showing me that pass receiving is understanding what I call the concept of separation, which is the ability of a receiver at that instant in which he makes a break or changes his direction to go from left to right or whatever, and to understand what the spatial relationship between himself and the defender is, and suddenly make a radical cut that creates instantaneous space—in other words, that gets him open. My objective was always to get into the end zone. And that's what Ray Renfro was able to teach me."

"What made Paul such a great receiver was the way he approached the game, the way he approached each player he played against," said Fair Hooker, a Browns receiver from 1969 to 1974. "He was very into the details of what they did, how they lined up. It was like a scientific evaluation of how he was going to attack those guys. He really did his homework."

As great as he was at catching the football, Warfield may have been even better at what he did *after* he caught the ball. "He had great hands, and I've never seen anyone run like him after the catch," said Bob Dolgan. "You could tell immediately that there was something special about him."

"He had those subtle moves that you really don't see where he can get a defensive back off balance and make the break," said ex–pro football executive Bobby Beathard in an NFL Films documentary on Warfield. "A lot of those great receivers have that. They don't just come down and break. They've done something in that move to get the guy off balance, and he was a master at that."

Recalled Raymond Berry, a Hall of Fame receiver for the Baltimore Colts from 1955 to 1967, of Warfield in the same documentary, "He just popped my eyes open watching him with his fluid movement . . . trying to cover the guy was a man-sized job because he had the great speed, but he could cut on a dime."

"It was fun to watch how smooth Warfield was and how graceful he was," Mike Peticca recalled. "You knew he could break a big play at any time. And, of course, Frank Ryan had the big arm that could hit him downfield pretty much just on go-routes in which he could outrun defensive backs. Then, with Bill Nelsen, I think they used him more as a medium-range receiver, although he was still a deep threat. It was just fun to watch him run with the ball after the catch. Also, what might be forgotten about him is that he was a really good blocker."

"Warfield reminded me of someone with wings almost," said Tom Melody. "When I'd go to Hiram for training camp, I loved to stand behind the offense and watch him run pass patterns. It seemed like he was gliding or floating. He was just so smooth. I don't know how you covered a guy like that, and obviously a lot of other people didn't either. He was a very gifted athlete."

Remembered Nelsen, "Blanton Collier said to me one time in the offseason, 'Bill, we've got to get the ball to Paul more.' I said, 'But if I throw the ball to [Gary] Collins, [Milt] Morin, and [Leroy] Kelly, that doesn't leave a whole lot left for Paul. I throw to him as much as I can.' He looked at me and said, 'Get the ball to Paul more.' So I tried to do that. Paul was really something. It was his glide, his natural speed, and he had a great little false step in fooling a defensive back, and then he was gone. He was tremendous that way."

The great Don Shula, Miami's head coach at the time, in the documentary on his former star, described Warfield in recalling a dazzling play he made against the Oakland Raiders on a Saturday night in 1970: "He caught a ball, broke away from some defenders, and did a pirouette, and got away, and got into the end zone . . . poetry in motion."

Warfield became a Hall of Famer despite playing for run-oriented teams. "That's quite a tribute to his greatness," said Ray Yannucci, a teammate of Warfield's at Warren G. Harding High School.

Warfield's fondest memory of his pro football days did not come during a game. Actually, it came prior to the Browns' *Monday Night Football* game against visiting Miami, where Warfield had been traded, on October 15, 1973. It was Warfield's first game in his old stomping grounds since getting dealt to the Dolphins three years earlier.

"Normally, at best, members of the opposition are politely booed," said Warfield. "The reception I got when introduced as a member of the Dolphins . . . I got a standing ovation! It was very emotional. It felt so good. It gave me chills. There's an old saying about 'how soon they forget,' but the reception I got that night was an indication to me that the fans in Cleveland really appreciated the years that I played there before going to Miami. It was an unbelievable feeling. It was indescribable."

AND THE WINNERS ARE . . .

Paul Warfield made it look so easy. His long strides after catching the ball were a sight to see. He was Jerry Rice before Jerry Rice. He is on the list of greatest Browns wide receivers of all time.

Dante Lavelli was nicknamed "Glue Fingers" for a reason—he almost never dropped the ball. Anything close to him, he caught. And he also had the knack for making clutch catches. He earns one of the spots for best Browns receivers ever.

How can we possibly have a Browns All-Time All-Star team without **Gary Collins** on it? Collins, like Lavelli, was known for making catches in crucial situations. He may not have had the most receptions in the league, but when the Browns needed a big play he was right there. Collins definitely gets voted as one of the team's greatest wide receivers ever.

WIDE RECEIVERS WHO DID NOT MAKE THE CUT

Reggie Rucker was not the fastest wide receiver ever, but he could get open and had great hands. He did not drop many balls. He was a good route runner, and Brian Sipe knew he was going to be where he was supposed to be. He was smart and adjusted his routes well based on what he saw and what he thought the quarterback was thinking. He wasn't necessarily a Pro Bowl type receiver, although he performed that way often. He was very, very above average. He was a very dependable player.

"He was a big-catch guy, a great player," Steve King said. "He was a player who Sipe looked for a lot because he had the ability to get open. He didn't have the big size but was fast, had good hands, and had good movement."

"Reggie was a heck of a wide receiver, he really was," added Ray Yannucci. "He was a very good athlete. He was also a very, very intelligent guy, an articulate guy. He graduated from Boston University, which is a really high intellectual school."

Dave Logan was actually drafted by the Browns out of the University of Colorado as a tight end, but he was misused his first couple of seasons with Cleveland. He wasn't big enough to be a tight end because of his weight, but he wasn't fast enough to be a wide receiver. He was really struggling playing both positions. He had no defined role. When Sam Rutigliano got the head-coaching job after the 1977 season he called Logan and said, "I'm going to move you from tight end to wide receiver."

"I remember Sam saying, 'I thought Logan was going to jump in through the phone line and kiss me' because he was so happy," remembered King. "The Browns were able to get a great tight end in Ozzie Newsome, and they needed another great receiver to go along with Reggie Rucker. Well, that guy became Dave Logan. And it really completely changed the Browns' offense in the late '70s. Logan made big catch after big catch.

Dave Logan celebrates a touchdown catch at home against the Colts on September 16, 1979 (PAUL TEPLEY/CLEVELAND STATE UNIVERSITY CLEVELAND PRESS ARCHIVES)

His memorable 46-yard touchdown reception late in the game against Green Bay in 1980 was the play of the season. They lose to Green Bay, and I don't know that they win the division. You talk about a guy who had maybe the best pair of hands a Browns player has ever had, and that's saying something."

Joe DeLamielleure will never forget Logan's TD catch against the Packers. "We won that game when he reached behind himself and pulled in the winning catch," he said. "That was probably one of the best catches I've ever seen. For a split second you thought, 'Ah, he's not gonna get it.' But he reached behind and grabbed that ball. He had the biggest hands in the world. He was unbelievable because of his hands. He made some big catches for us."

"Dave was one of my favorites," said Mike McLain. "He made one of the great catches I ever saw when he one-handed the ball over Mel Blount of the Steelers at Three Rivers Stadium."

"He was fun to watch," added Mike Peticca. "He had great size. He was a great basketball and baseball player and obviously a special football player, so he was a great athlete. With his size and athleticism, look at the various spots to where Sipe got the ball to him as far as how Logan's body was situated. You get the ball within a certain radius of him, and he's got a great chance to make the catch."

Brian Brennan would have been the hero had John Elway not taken a "Sunday Drive" to Pasadena.

"He would've had the catch that put the Browns in the Super Bowl," Jeff Schudel said. "He wasn't the biggest guy by far, but boy, he played with all his heart. He should be remembered very fondly by Browns fans."

"Here was a guy who couldn't run down the field," said King, "and he almost made the play of the '86 season when he catches the touchdown pass in the AFC Championship Game when he turned Dennis Smith into 'Mr. Pretzel.'"

"Bernie [Kosar] threw a duck," laughed Brennan. "I think he'd look to me in one-on-one situations where Webster Slaughter and I were always on the same side of the ball, or a lot of the time. And the defense liked to double cover Webster, and that puts the free safety, or strong safety, or the nickel back, more on me, so it was always a good matchup for Bernie."

Kosar saw that Smith was one-on-one with Brennan on the touchdown pass in the Denver game. "I remember the play—catching the pass and going into the end zone—was a special moment for me," Brennan said. "Here I am, a chance to shine without Doug Flutie [his main college quarterback]. I remember coming over to the sideline and almost shaking with excitement, standing next to Gary Danielson and just hoping and believing we were going to the Super Bowl."

"Brennan caught everything and was physically tough," said Peticca. "He might've had that stereotype as a possession receiver, but I thought he also had to be really respected on the medium-deep routes."

Brennan always had a chip on his shoulder. He always resented the fact that people didn't think he was all that fast. Said Mike McLain, "Being his size and not being a highly-touted prospect was probably the best thing for him."

"I was proud to have played in Cleveland, and it was a privilege to play for the Cleveland Browns organization and the Cleveland Browns' fans," Brennan said. "Football means a great deal to these fans, and they deserve the best product."

There was nothing about **Reggie Langhorne**, even when he played in bits and pieces in his rookie season of 1985, that would have led anyone to believe that he was going to be a great wide receiver.

"You credit Langhorne for developing into that receiver between '85 and '86, and you credit Lindy Infante for developing an offense that utilized his talents," said King. "Every day in the week leading up to the game at Cincinnati in '86 that was basically for the AFC Central Division title, Kosar went to Marty Schottenheimer and said, 'Let's throw the bomb on the first play.' Schottenheimer would say, 'Ahhh, I don't know.' Marty softened up as the week went on. So finally on Friday when Kosar said to Schottenheimer, 'Let's throw the bomb on the first play,' Marty said, 'You know what? I'll think about it.' And on the very first play from scrimmage, Kosar threw that bomb down the right sideline to Langhorne. It was completed for 66 yards down to the one-yard line. Three plays later Kevin Mack scored, and the Browns were up 7-0 before the people in Riverfront were even in their seats. The Browns went on to clobber the Bengals, 34-3. That play to Langhorne just blew the doors off of the Bengals' corners. Langhorne was a great player and a tough player, too."

"Reggie was a big, fast receiver," said Ray Yannucci. "He was excellent."

"He was a good, tough wide receiver," Doug Dieken said.

Webster Slaughter made a name for himself right off the bat in his rookie season.

"Webster was probably one of the best wide receivers the Browns have had," said Yannucci. "He was very, very good, an excellent player. He was a cocky guy—but not derogatorily—and I think that helped him be the player he was."

"Slaughter had probably the quickest release I've ever seen from a receiver," McLain said. "That first step of his was fantastic. He had great hands. For a second-round pick, he was superb."

"Webster was a talented guy," said Dieken. "He was a good receiver."

"You go back and look at that receiving core that Bernie had, they were pretty good," said Yannucci. "Now they weren't Hall of Fame caliber or All-Pro caliber, but as a combination they were fantastic."

Langhorne was a perfect complement to Slaughter. Slaughter was the deep threat that the Browns did not have before. He opened things up across the middle and opened up the running game. But to do that, you have to have players go across the middle and catch the ball, and they had that in Langhorne.

"You can't say 'Slaughter' without saying 'Langhorne' and 'Brennan,' and vice versa," McLain said. "They were like the Three Musketeers. They came as a group set. That was as good of a three-receiver set as any team has had probably in the history of the league."

"With Bernie throwing them the ball, that was a pretty unstoppable offense," said Schudel. "They gave a lot of headaches to opposing coaches."

"All those guys had such great hands," said Peticca.

"That whole crew—Slaughter, Langhorne, and Brennan—found a chemistry that remained successful for quite a few years," Dieken said.

Jarvis Landry came to the Browns when it wasn't cool. He arrived in Cleveland when the Browns were coming off 1-15 and 0-16 seasons, respectively. He was willing to go to the Browns and be a leader on a team that was just terrible. "There was the question about him tearing those guys apart in the locker room one day for their lack of professionalism and preparedness. Well, that was Jarvis Landry," said King. "That was who he was, who he is. I have tremendous respect for him. I am so happy for him that this team has won lately because he kind of helped start it, helped ignite it, helped give them a little bit of something solid that you could count on when they really didn't have much. I'm so happy that he's been able to reap the benefits of that. You talk about a team guy, Jarvis Landry is a team guy. He could've existed and played in any era."

"It's no secret that the Browns suddenly got good because they have a guy like Jarvis Landry," said McLain. "If he caught two passes all season, he'd still be useful in the locker room and around his teammates. Everybody needs a Jarvis Landry on their team."

"Jarvis has some of the best hands I've ever seen," Dieken said. "He's a guy you want on your team. You know you're going to get a hundred percent from him every game. He comes to play. He's a blue-collar wide receiver. He's not afraid to block, either. I have a lot of respect for Jarvis."

"You look at the passion he plays with," said Schudel. "He takes such pride in the way he plays."

DEFENSE

ENDS

The Candidates

Len Ford
Bill Glass
Jack Gregory
Myles Garrett

A great right defensive end for the Browns from 1950 to 1957, Len Ford made life miserable for opposing quarterbacks. He started every game from 1951 to 1956. He recovered a fumble in the end zone for a touchdown in a 49–7 win over the Eagles on October 19, 1952. He was First-Team All-Pro and a Pro Bowler from 1951 to 1954. He was enshrined in the Pro Football Hall of Fame in 1976.

Playing mostly left defensive end for the Browns from 1957 to 1967 was Paul Wiggin. Wiggin had 60.5 sacks in his career. His best sack totals were nine in 1960 and 8.5 in both 1964 and 1967 (even though sacks did not become an official NFL statistic until 1982, teams still kept sack totals prior to that, and those prior sack totals for the Browns are used in this book). He was a member of the 1964 Browns NFL championship team that shut out the Baltimore Colts 27–0 in the title game. He returned an interception 20 yards for a touchdown in a 48–34 win over the New York Giants on December 18,

1960. He returned a fumble 2 yards for a touchdown in a 42–20 triumph over the Giants on October 25, 1964. He was a Pro Bowler in 1965 and 1967.

A right defensive end for Cleveland from 1962 to 1968, Bill Glass was a monster when it came to getting to the quarterback. He totaled 77.5 sacks with the Browns. He had 16.5 sacks in 1965, 15.5 sacks in 1962, and 15 sacks in 1966. He returned a fumble 13 yards for a touchdown in a 49–40 win over the Giants on December 4, 1966. He returned an interception 2 yards for a score in a 24–10 victory over the Saints on September 15, 1968. He was a member of the 1964 NFL championship Browns team. Glass was picked for the Pro Bowl from 1962 to 1964 and in 1967.

Playing right defensive end for Cleveland from 1967 to 1971 and in 1979 was Jack Gregory. Gregory sacked the quarterback 41 times as a Brown. He had 15.5 sacks in 1970 and 11 in 1969. He was a Pro Bowler in 1969.

Carl Hairston played mostly right defensive end for the Browns from 1984 to 1989. He had 37.5 sacks with the Browns. He had nine sacks in 1986, eight in 1987, and seven in 1985. He was a major part of a Browns defense that helped the team to five straight postseason berths.

A left defensive end for Cleveland from 1990 to 1995, Rob Burnett had 40.5 sacks with the Browns. His high was 10 sacks in 1994, his lone Pro Bowl season. He had nine sacks in both 1992 and 1993. He was a big part of a Browns defense that led the team to the playoffs and yielded the fewest points in the league in 1994.

Myles Garrett has proven worthy of his being the number one overall pick by the Browns in the 2017 NFL Draft. He has a knack for getting to the quarterback. He has amassed 58.5 sacks since his rookie season of 2017, and that was with missing several games. He had 16 sacks in 2021, 13.5 sacks in 2018,

12 sacks in 2020, 10 sacks in 2019, and seven sacks in 2017. He was First-Team All-Pro in 2020 and was picked for the Pro Bowl in 2018 and in 2020 and 2021.

Those in the running for best defensive ends in Browns history are Ford, Glass, Gregory, and Garrett.

LEN FORD

Len Ford was a destroyer. He was big, strong, fast, tough, an unbelievable physical specimen.

"He had the ability to move quickly and just be a brute force at the point of attack," said Steve King. "What a great defensive line he played on. When you think of the Browns' defense in the 1940s and '50s, which was tremendous but got overshadowed by the offense, you can look to Ford and middle guard Bill Willis as being shining examples of that, two great players. Ford had been a wide receiver with the Los Angeles Dons in the AAFC, so the Browns knew all about him. When the league folded and was absorbed into the NFL and the Dons went away, Paul Brown remembered that and went out and signed him, and it turned into a great signing. For eight years, Ford was just a rock at defensive end. You can't say enough good things about Len Ford."

"Len was feared by most quarterbacks," said Jim Ray Smith.

"He was a great defensive end, one of the greatest," Bob Dolgan said.

BILL GLASS

Bill Glass demonstrated toughness and a great pass-rushing ability.

"Bill was a key part of our defensive line," recalled Paul Warfield, "in that he always had the ability to come up and make key sacks of quarterbacks and had the great athletic ability to move off the ball with quickness yet had the ability to change directions. He was an instrumental part of the success of our defensive unit."

"Glass was a great pass rusher," Steve King said. "His sack totals show you what a dominant defensive end he was. He was at his best in the '64 championship game. He was dominating, he was in John Unitas's face all day long, he just would not be denied."

Said Fred Hoaglin, "Bill was a tremendous, tremendous pass rusher."

JACK GREGORY

It took a while for Jack Gregory to adapt to his position with the Browns.

"I played in a 5-4 defense in college where it was a standup defense," he explained. "A 5-4 lineman plays like a linebacker. The Browns put me in a left-handed stance in the 4-3 alignment that I'd never played in the down position. I'm right-handed. It was a great adjustment."

As a rookie, Gregory was tested right off the bat in the 1967 Pro Football Hall of Fame Game against the Philadelphia Eagles. "My first opposition was Bob Brown," he remembered, "so you can understand that it was a tough deal. Paul Wiggin's advice was, 'Stay low.'"

"Jack was a complete player," said Billy Andrews. "Not only was he a great pass rusher, he was a terrific run stopper."

"Gregory, I thought, was a better-than-average defensive end," said Mike McLain. "At various times, he was one of the better pass rushers the Browns have had."

"What happened offensively overshadowed it," Mike Peticca added, "but something you can't overlook about the 1968 Browns team was that it might've been one of the better Browns' defensive teams of that era. And it might've been one of the best Browns' big-play defenses during that era. Gregory was only in his second season but made a big impact when Bill Glass was out with an injury."

Gregory wanted to stay with the Browns after the 1971 season, but he and Art Modell were $1,500 apart contract-wise. "Nowadays, that's chump change," said Steve King. "They couldn't agree on a contract, and Gregory went and signed with the New York Giants and became a great defensive end through most of the '70s. He came back to the Browns in 1979, but by that time he was just a shadow of himself. Modell not wanting to give him $1,500 cost the Browns because when Bill Glass and Paul Wiggin retired, they were looking for defensive ends throughout the '70s. Nobody they had in the '70s was like a Jack Gregory, nobody was even close. Just think what that line might've been with Jerry Sherk at tackle and Jack Gregory at defensive end. Now there's one half of a very, very good defensive line. And when Walter Johnson was there, it would've been three-fourths of a very good line. All those great seasons Gregory had with the Giants should've been with the Browns."

"I was really disappointed when they lost Gregory," said Peticca. "He was emerging as one of the best pass rushers in the league. He was a guy who could change the game with one play."

MYLES GARRETT

Myles Garrett is a physical freak of nature.

"The way his ankles bend when he's going around an offensive tackle to get to the quarterback," said Jeff Schudel, "nobody should be able to do that, but he does. The way he works out . . . he's everything he was supposed to be as that number one draft pick."

"He's as solid as they come," Doug Dieken said. "He reminds me a little bit of Lee Roy Selmon. As far as athletic defensive ends, Lee Roy was good."

Number one overall draft pick Myles Garrett during training camp in his 2017 rookie season (TRACY EVANS/DREAMSTIME.COM)

For all the things that the Browns did wrong over the last 20 years—and you could write a book about them—the one thing they did right was draft Garrett. Garrett came to the Browns with the reputation of being a great pass-rusher, and he is. He did it those first couple of years with no help from any of his teammates. The Browns did not have much talent then. "You see him just dominate tackles," said Steve King. "You don't see that much anymore because they've liberalized the passing rules so much that the offensive guy has all the breaks in terms of rules that keep a defensive guy out of the backfield. But this guy can do it. He gets double- and even triple-teamed. Now, the Browns have some very good players along the defensive line, so if teams want to double- and triple-team Garrett, go ahead, fine. They've got other guys now who can wreak havoc. Garrett is always going to be remembered for what happened against Pittsburgh [in 2019 when he slammed quarterback Mason Rudolph's head with Rudolph's own helmet]. He has to do something so big and so grand that the incident with Rudolph gets pushed to page two, and I really think he's going to do that."

"The speed Garrett has and his ability to get low at that size has to be scary for offensive tackles," Mike McLain said. "I think what he did in 2020 while he clearly was dragging from coming back from Covid and not having a complementary pass rusher makes his season even better. He's clearly one of the most dominant players in the league now."

And the Winners Are . . .

Len Ford was as good as they come when it comes to defensive ends. He was powerful, he had strength, and he had speed. He no doubt takes one of the spots for best Browns defensive ends of all time.

Bill Glass nudges out Myles Garrett for the other spot for greatest Browns defensive ends ever. The reason? Quite simply, Garrett has not played enough games to warrant him being on our all-time team.

ENDS WHO DID NOT MAKE THE CUT

Paul Wiggin was a major contributor to the success of the Browns of the late 1950s and 1960s. "He was our team captain and a true leader in that sense," said Paul Warfield. "He had the capacity and ability to put it all together, to emphasize what we needed as a team. Much like Blanton Collier, he wasn't a yeller, he wasn't a screamer. In very conversational tones, he could get the message to all of us. His leadership was ideal, and I had great respect for him. He was an excellent player in addition to that."

"Wiggin and Bill Glass, they don't get the credit they deserve because they were really the best pair of defensive ends the Browns have ever had. They were just outstanding," said Steve King.

"Paul never did anything flashy but always did what he was supposed to do," Jim Kanicki said.

"You knew he was on the field. He was a presence," said Tom Melody. "He was also a very bright guy."

The late 1980s Browns teams were known for their offense, but their defense was a pretty good unit, and **Carl Hairston** was a huge part of it.

"It was just great playing with Sam Clancy, Bob Golic, Clay Matthews . . . guys like that," said Hairston. "We had some talented players. Our corners were two of the best in the league in bump-and-run, which gave us [the defensive line] more time to rush the passer."

"Hairston would shed those blockers," Jeff Schudel said. "The Browns' run defense was pretty good in those days, and 'Big Daddy' was a big part of that."

"He was a heck of a football player," said Ray Yannucci. "He was one of the best defensive players the Browns had during that time. He was really tough."

"Carl was a real good player," said Joe DeLamielleure. "He was a leader. A lot of guys looked up to him. I wasn't surprised when he became a coach because he was smart."

Rob Burnett went from being undersized his rookie season to the next year being one of the better defensive ends in the NFL. "Burnett had one of the biggest transformations in his body from year one to year two," Mike McLain recalled. "That really made him a dependable, good player. I didn't think he was going to make it to be honest, but he worked his way into becoming a good player."

Bill Belichick purged a lot of players off the 1990 team when he took over as head coach in 1991, but one guy he did not get rid of was Burnett. "That's because Burnett could play. There was no question about it, he was a great player," said King. "In 1994, when the Browns went to the playoffs, he and Anthony Pleasant were the cornerstones of a very good defensive line that also had Michael Dean Perry. Burnett was very confident in his own abilities. He never doubted the fact that he could make it in the league, make it big in the league. He was a real pro's pro. He was a smooth player, consistently good."

TACKLES

Lou Rymkus
Bob Gain
Walter Johnson
Jerry Sherk
Michael Dean Perry

Lou Rymkus was a very solid right defensive tackle for the Browns from 1946 to 1951, an integral part of so many great Cleveland defenses of the late 1940s and early 1950s. He was dependable, too, rarely ever missing a game.

John Kissell played left defensive tackle for the Browns from 1950 to 1952 and 1954 to 1956. He was a key part of three NFL championship teams—in 1950, 1954, and 1955. On top of that, he never missed a game.

Manning mostly left defensive tackle for the Browns in 1952 and from 1954 to 1964 was Bob Gain. Gain was a cornerstone on some fine Browns teams in the late 1950s and early 1960s. He had 5.5 sacks in 1961 and four in 1962. He returned an interception 22 yards for a touchdown in a 48–34 victory over the Giants on December 18, 1960. He was a Pro Bowler from 1957 to 1959 and in 1961 and 1962.

Don Colo played mainly right defensive tackle for Cleveland from 1953 to 1958. He was a big part of teams that won NFL titles in 1954 and 1955. He never missed a game. He was picked for the Pro Bowl in 1954, 1955, and 1958.

Jim Kanicki in action against Dallas in the late 1960s (PAUL TEPLEY/ CLEVELAND STATE UNIVERSITY CLEVELAND PRESS ARCHIVES)

Playing right defensive tackle from 1963 to 1969, Jim Kanicki totaled 24.5 sacks with Cleveland. He had 7.5 sacks in 1968 and 5.5 sacks in 1966. Perhaps Kanicki's best game ever was the 1964 championship game in which the Browns shocked the Colts 27–0.

A left defensive tackle for the Browns from 1964 to 1966, Dick Modzelewski brought great talent and veteran leadership to a pretty young team, and he played a major role in the Browns winning the NFL championship in 1964 and getting to the title game in 1965. He had 7.5 sacks in 1965. He was a Pro Bowler in 1964.

Walter Johnson was a tremendous left defensive tackle for Cleveland from 1965 to 1976. He totaled 66 sacks for the Browns, with eight sacks in both 1969 and 1972 and 7.5 sacks in 1967. He never missed a game. He returned two fumbles for touchdowns, both against New Orleans—a 12-yarder in a 27–17 win on October 12, 1969, and an end zone recovery in a 21–17 win on December 12, 1971. He was a Pro Bowler from 1967 to 1969.

From 1970 to 1981, Jerry Sherk was as good as they come when it comes to right defensive tackles. He had great power, speed, and agility. He amassed a total of 70.5 sacks in his career. He had a dozen sacks in both 1976 and 1979. The latter year, he was having perhaps his finest season ever until he suffered a serious staph infection in Week 10 at Philadelphia that ended his season and, for all intents and purposes, his career. He was First-Team All-Pro in 1976 and was a Pro Bowler from 1973 to 1976.

Michael Dean Perry played right defensive tackle for the Browns from 1988 to 1994. He was a fabulous talent. He totaled 51.5 sacks with the Browns with a high of 11.5 in 1990. He had 8.5 sacks in both 1991 and 1992. He returned a fumble 10 yards for a touchdown in the Browns' 28–23 victory over

Houston on December 18, 1988, a win that put the Browns in the playoffs. He was the UPI AFC Defensive MVP in 1989. He was First-Team All-Pro in 1989 and 1990 and a Pro Bowler from 1989 to 1991 and in 1993 and 1994.

The players who have a shot at being one of the best defensive tackles in Browns history are Rymkus, Gain, Johnson, Sherk, and Perry.

LOU RYMKUS

Lou Rymkus was probably the first great defensive tackle the Browns ever had. Back in the 1940s and early '50s with their great defenses, it started up front, and Rymkus was the man then.

"Rymkus was a guy who probably not too many Browns fans think about, maybe they've never even heard of, but he was a tremendous player," said Steve King. "The only thing that was his problem was that he was on the opposite side of the ball of a great offensive team. He got overshadowed. You look at how many points the Browns scored in those days, but look at how few points they gave up, and a lot of that was because of guys like Lou Rymkus. Nobody talks about it because it was a billion years ago, but he was a real key member of those early Browns teams that were so good."

BOB GAIN

Bob Gain was a borderline Hall of Famer.

"He was a great football player," Steve King said. "He had the ability to play well, and he also spoke what he felt. He told a story of him going to Paul Brown and saying, 'Hey, you can't be so reactive to everything the guys are doing. Let us play our game, let us be ourselves, and we can beat the Giants.' He was not afraid to tell Brown that. Outside of Jerry Sherk and maybe Michael Dean Perry, Gain is the third best defensive tackle the

Browns have ever had. He was a key player on great defenses that played in key games and won championships."

"We had a great group of guys," said Gain. "They knew how to win, and they knew how to go after people. You know, everybody thought we were a finesse team. That was a lot of baloney. We could play with any of 'em. We were as tough as they were."

When asked about the Browns' 38–14 rout of the Rams in Los Angeles in the 1955 NFL championship game, Gain said, "They [the Rams] were bragging, saying we were all fat cats, that we'd won it the year before. They were poppin' off about it, saying, 'We'll take Cleveland without any trouble.' Well, we went out there and went into a double wing and we just ruined 'em."

After that title game, the Los Angeles Touchdown Club named Gain its NFL Defensive Player of the Year.

"Bob was very proud of that," said Dan Coughlin.

Gain broke his right leg in a game early in 1964, ending his season. "It was heartbreaking having to sit out most of that championship year," he said. "But things happen. I remember when the fans honored me down at the stadium in 1964, it was a really warm affair. Every section, we went by in a golf cart—I had my leg in a cast—and everybody stood up and applauded. It was very emotional . . . very, very emotional."

WALTER JOHNSON
Walter Johnson commanded respect.

In 1975, near the end of Johnson's career, head coach Forrest Gregg wanted to see what kind of guard Robert E. Jackson was. Jackson was a rookie and came out of nowhere, and Gregg liked him. Gregg put Jackson out there to see what he could do against Johnson.

"So they go one on one," said Steve King, who was told the story by Doug Dieken. "Now Johnson's forearms were like tree trunks. The first play, Walter comes up with that forearm of his and pops Jackson in the jaw and knocks him backwards and he staggers back. They do this three or four times, and Jackson is just getting the snot beat out of him, is just getting pounded by Johnson. To Jackson's credit, he was never KO'd. And that's what made Gregg keep a roster spot for him, the fact that he could stand in there and not win but just survive against Walter Johnson. Johnson was a bear. Everyone respected Walter."

"Walter Johnson was a huge man," remembered Paul Warfield. "Offensive teams were unable to penetrate or run inside against him. He was tough to move, he was aggressive, a very strong player. He had a very quiet personality but was very effective against the run game."

"He was strong," Mike Pruitt said. "I'll never forget when he collared me at practice one time, and I'm thinking, 'Man, nobody ever hit me around the neck and head!' He said, 'Welcome to the NFL, rookie.'"

Johnson had been having a problem with his right hand, so he got a Novocain shot prior to the NFL championship game in Minnesota on January 4, 1970. "His right hand was the one he put down on the ground in his three-point stance," recalled Dan Coughlin. "And, because of the Novocain in his hand, he didn't feel his hand freezing and it froze. Later, while the team is at the airport waiting to fly back to Cleveland, the Novocain wears off Walter's hand, and as it wears off, his hand also is defrosting! The pain suddenly was agonizing. Big Walter Johnson crumpled down to the concourse floor. An ambulance hauled him to a hospital in Minneapolis, and he spent several days there. They saved his hand."

Another memory regarding Johnson occurred almost three years later on November 19, 1972, a day in which the Browns defeated the Steelers in a crucial game, 26–24, on a late Don Cockroft field goal in Municipal Stadium.

"Everyone's hootin' and hollerin' and whatever," King said, "and Walter Johnson walked in the locker room and said, 'What are you guys doin'?' And the players said, 'We're celebrating.' Walter says, 'We've got to go play those guys again in two weeks. Let's settle down and let's be pros about this.' And that was Walter Johnson. 'You want to celebrate a little bit, fine, but don't carry it on. We've got a season to play.' And that's the kind of professional Walter Johnson was."

JERRY SHERK

Jerry Sherk's wrestling career at Oklahoma State University helped him when he got to the NFL.

"I had developed a good workout ethic because wrestlers are maniacs," he said. "I used balance and conditioning more than others. The Browns didn't have much of a weight room when I got there, so I did a lot of push-ups and sit-ups and running. Being a wrestler also helped me with the mental part of the game. I imagined during games that it was just me and that guy across from me—and this really helped. Also, for some reason, I really 'wanted it.' I wanted to do well and hear the cheers."

Sherk had a good mind—an analytic one—for the game of football with or without wrestling. "I could see what it took to be successful," he said. "Very often, the formula was simple—get in better shape than anyone and be aggressive on each and every play, even if we were losing, 30–0, which we often were."

Dick Modzelewski, Sherk's defensive line coach the first part of his career, was a former defensive tackle, so he knew what it took. He knew exactly how to handle Sherk. He would leave him in games as a rookie, even when it was hurting the team somewhat. "He would tell me, 'I'm leaving you in so your confidence won't be broken, and this will even help the team in the long run,'" recalled Sherk. "There are few coaches with that kind of intuition and feel for the game and the players they are coaching."

It took a few years for Sherk to adapt to the NFL game. "I took lots of bumps at first," he said. "You feel like you're a target when you're young and inexperienced. Helmets kept hitting me full force in those early days. Later, *I* became the missile, putting my helmet on running backs almost at will."

Sherk will never forget the Browns' 20–14 defeat at unbeaten Miami in an AFC divisional playoff on Christmas Eve 1972. "I was fired up for that game," he said. "I remember I was so excited that I didn't settle down until the second quarter. I told myself at the time that there's getting too up for a game, and that I wouldn't let that happen again."

"Jerry's a student of the game, he always studied it. Everybody looked up to him," said Modzelewski. "He not only was the best tackle I ever coached, he was also the smartest."

Mentor actually learned from student.

"Jerry taught me about extending the arms and coming off the ball with full extension," Modzelewski remembered. "He had separation between him and the offensive player. Today's linemen come off the ball standing straight up, chest to chest, instead of full extension. Jerry was slow in the 40-yard dash, but all I cared about was how fast he was within 10 yards. He was quick from his position to the quarterback. He hustled all the time, in practice too. He'd pursue players and chase them down."

"When I rejoined the Browns in 1976, Jerry Sherk, along with Walter Johnson, were the most formidable part of the defense," said Paul Warfield. "Jerry was not as big or strong as Walter, but nevertheless he could defend his position and solidify and hold his ground. In addition to that, he was quicker, had an explosion off the ball, so he was very difficult for centers and also guards offensively to block because he could slide and he could move off the ball so quickly. He presented maximum problems. He had a very fine career. He was an excellent player."

"Jerry was quick, probably one of the best defensive ends who you could have," said Mike Pruitt. "He would get around those linemen so quick that they wouldn't even touch him! When his knee got messed up is what really slowed him down, and he was not the same Jerry Sherk."

What Pruitt was speaking of was the serious staph infection Sherk suffered in a game at Philadelphia on November 4, 1979. He almost lost his life from it. The injury, in effect, ended his career.

"If that staph infection hadn't happened, I think he could've actually gone on to a Hall of Fame career," Jeff Schudel said.

"For my money, Sherk should be in the Hall of Fame," said Steve King. "He was having the best season of his career in '79 when he had that staph infection. He was off the charts. He went from that to almost losing his life. And, really, that was the end of his career. Had he been able to play a year or two more, I think he'd be in the Hall of Fame. He did not benefit from being on very good teams. The Browns in the 1970s, of course, were not good, but Jerry Sherk was a Pro Bowl player. He prepared like a Pro Bowler, too. In one of the Pro Bowls in the early to mid-'70s, Sherk and L.C. Greenwood of Pittsburgh were on the same side of the line. It was a play down near the AFC goal line. Sherk and Greenwood both got cut at the line of scrimmage. Greenwood just laid there and didn't move. Well, Sherk—and this was a Pro Bowl, not the playoffs—got up and chased the runner down from the opposite side and stopped him from scoring a touchdown!

"I remember Sherk telling me that the game of football for him slowed down so much that it almost was like slow motion to him. He could just see things and read things. There were a lot of times when opposing teams thought he had jumped the snap count and was in the backfield too soon, had jumped offside. But Sherk *hadn't* jumped offsides. His first step was so quick and so fast, he penetrated into the backfield so quickly that it *looked* like he was offside. His technique was impeccable. He was tremendously intelligent. He was just a great player."

"He's maybe one of my five favorite players in Browns history," Mike McLain said. "Not too many Browns could've started on Pittsburgh's 'Steel Curtain,' but he could've. He was that good of a player. He was so quick, so strong. When he was healthy and at his best, he dominated people. He was a Hall of Fame talent."

MICHAEL DEAN PERRY

Marty Schottenheimer, for whatever reasons, did not want the Browns to draft Michael Dean Perry in 1988.

They drafted him anyway.

"He had to fight his way on to the team," said Steve King. "Towards the end of his rookie season in '88, he was making some big plays, especially in the playoff-clinching, last game of the regular season against Houston and the playoff game against Houston the next week. That was a guy who should've been playing from the moment he stepped on to the training camp field. He was just an unbelievable player. He had a great first step and got into the backfield very quickly. You didn't see him celebrating and doing all of that jumping up and down. He just played. He was a load. He played with some bad teams during the first part of the '90s, but you never saw him give up."

Perry was a legitimately sensational player. He made such an impact against the run game and scaring the quarterback. "Teams had to game-plan for him," Mike Peticca said. "I don't know how many players defensively, even though the Browns had a lot of good players defensively, they had that teams really had to game-plan for as far as trying to defend a great player. Perry was truly a great player."

"Michael Dean was a really, really quick defensive tackle," said Doug Dieken. "He had leverage because he was shorter."

"His ability to just shoot gaps was amazing," added Mike McLain. "His quickness was what stood out to me."

AND THE WINNERS ARE . . .

It was really a shame that **Jerry Sherk** suffered the staph infection in 1979. Had he played a few more seasons while healthy, he most likely would be in the Pro Football Hall of Fame. He no doubt fills one of the spots as greatest Browns defensive tackles ever.

Walter Johnson not only could get to the quarterback, he could stop the run. He could do it all. He edges out Michael Dean Perry for the other spot as one of the team's greatest defensive tackles ever.

TACKLES WHO DID NOT MAKE THE CUT

John Kissell was a mainstay on those exceptional, early Browns defenses.

"He was a great player, a real pro's pro," said Steve King. "When you look at what those defenses did, they didn't get nearly the credit they deserved, and guys like Kissell were reasons why. They were just as good as the offense was, but when you have future Hall of Famers on the offense, nobody notices the defense. Nobody buys tickets to go watch John Kissell stuff the run."

"John was a strong tackle," Jim Ray Smith said.

Don Colo was a good, solid tackle.

"He was the second great defensive tackle the Browns ever had," said King. "He's another name that a lot of Browns fans don't remember. He was just a very, very good tackle, very consistent. He was a big man but also an athletic guy. Paul Brown liked a guy like Don Colo. He knew he wasn't flashy, but he knew he could count on him."

"Colo had a reputation of being a real tough character," said Bob Dolgan.

Jim Kanicki was a big, strong, tough guy.

"He made major contributions certainly in the defensive rush and was a very, very good player," Paul Warfield said.

"Kanicki was a good run stopper," said Mike Peticca. "He was really solid."

"Jim was just a powerful guy. He had big arms," Dick Modzelewski said.

"He was also a good guy to have on the team, a good locker room guy," said Paul Wiggin.

Kanicki was tremendous in the 1964 championship game win over Baltimore. He was up against Jim Parker, a premier guard. But Kanicki was a big guy, and it created a stalemate. "Parker had his hands full with him," said King.

"Parker could not control him," Dan Coughlin added. "That might've been the highlight of Jim Kanicki's career."

Dick Modzelewski's background as a player for the New York Giants for many years really helped younger players on the Browns when he was traded to the team in 1964.

"I think it inspired them," said Peticca. "Even though he wasn't quite the player he once was, if you were watching him out there in the middle of the Browns' defensive line, the guy who'd truly been a great player certainly wasn't going to get fooled, and if he ever got beat on anything it was because he was getting older. The intangibles he brought were priceless."

"Dick knew where everybody on the defensive line should be," said Kanicki. "I think the 1963 season [when the Browns started 6-0 but finished 10-4] taught everybody a lesson about not resting on your laurels. You learn from that. We had good, veteran players. I think we had great leadership, too, especially when we brought in Dick. In fact, Dick kind of took me under his wing to settle me down because he said I was too aggressive."

"Coming from the Giants, Dick knew about winning," Warfield said. "He was very helpful to our success."

"Dick was a very established football player," said Wiggin. "He was very fundamental, very solid, a good player. He was also a great guy to have on your team. He was full of personality and everybody liked him."

NOSE TACKLE

THE CANDIDATES

Bill Willis
Bob Golic

Bill Willis began his career at right guard but was switched to nose tackle for the rest of his career, which lasted from 1946 to 1953. He was really a middle guard. Back then, all teams had a five-man front. There were two ends, two tackles, and a middle guard over the center, and that was Willis. The modern nose tackle is a squatty, physical guy who looks like a sumo wrestler. Willis was certainly not that. Back in the 1940s and '50s, when they stood up that middle guard, he ended up being a middle linebacker. That is the kind of athletic player the middle guards were back in the day. And Willis was perfect for that, a tremendously athletic guy. He defined the position, which disappeared with the advent of the 4-3 defense shortly after his retirement. He was a key component to several great Browns defenses. He was First-Team All-Pro from 1951 to 1953 and a Pro Bowler from 1950 to 1953. He was enshrined in the Pro Football Hall of Fame in 1977.

After playing linebacker for New England his first three seasons in the NFL, Bob Golic was traded to the Browns, for whom he played nose tackle from 1982 to 1988. He was a very talented player who was a member of some fine Browns defenses that helped the team to several playoff berths. He returned his only career interception 7 yards for a touchdown in a 35–21 loss to Green Bay on November 6, 1983. He totaled 14 sacks as a Brown with a high of four in 1982. He was a Pro Bowler from 1985 to 1987.

Ahtyba Rubin was a solid nose tackle for Cleveland from 2008 to 2014. He played for some very poor Browns teams but seemingly never took a play off. He amassed 12 career sacks as a Brown with a high of five in 2011.

The two players in the running for greatest Browns nose tackle of all time are Willis and Golic.

BILL WILLIS

Bill Willis was coaching at Kentucky State College when Paul Brown became head coach of the Browns. Willis was planning on playing for the Montreal Alouettes of the CFL.

"The Sunday before the Monday I was to go to Canada, I got a call from a newspaper reporter by the name of Paul Hornung of the *Columbus Dispatch*," recalled Willis in the December 2006 edition of the *Orange and Brown Report*. "He happened to be a personal friend of Paul Brown. He literally guaranteed that I would make the [Browns] team. He was so insistent. He said, 'Why don't you stop by on your way to Canada? Just stop by.' So I did stop by Bowling Green [State University, the site of the Browns' training camp then]. Paul [Brown] saw me walking across the field and said, 'Go to the training room and get suited up.' We had a practice the next day, and during that practice, Paul put me in front of [center] Mo Scarry, who had played on the championship Cleveland Rams. When the ball was snapped, I charged and they weren't able to run a play. About four or five times, I would charge and either disrupt the ball before it got to Otto Graham or I was around

Graham's neck before he could get out from underneath the center. [Brown] got on either end of the line of scrimmage to see if I was offside. I was not offside. I just lined up as close as I could to the center. If the center just pushed his thumb a little bit, got ready to center the ball, I'd charge."

"Scarry said, 'What the hell happened?'" Bob Dolgan remembered. "So Scarry does it again on the next play, and the same thing happens. He snapped the ball and Willis knocks down Scarry and grabs Graham. And Scarry said to the coaches, 'Hey, what the hell is going on here? He's charging before the ball is snapped, isn't he?' The coaches said, 'No, he's just that fast.' Willis was just a tremendous middle guard."

Willis made the ballclub. The rest is history. Incidentally, it was years later that Willis found out that Brown had put Hornung up to calling him.

"In practice," said Steve King, "Willis would literally jump over, leap over, Frank Gatski to go into the backfield and make the play! And Gatski would be screaming, 'Hey, he can't do that!' That's how good Willis was."

In a 1950 playoff game against the Giants, with the Browns leading, 6–3, in the fourth quarter, the Giants' Charlie "Choo" Roberts, probably the fastest player in the league, peeled off a big run. "Willis had been chop-blocked, cut down at the line of scrimmage, on the play," King said. "Willis is laying on the ground 10-12 yards behind Roberts. Willis gets up and chases Roberts down at the seven-yard line, saving the touchdown. As it turned out, the Giants didn't get any points. That was the play of the game. The Browns won, 8-3. Willis was asked how he did it, and he said, 'The runner was carrying a football, but I saw him carrying a bag of money that belonged to me,' and that was the playoff money the Browns would've won by beating the Giants and advancing to the championship game. Back then, that playoff money helped quite a bit heading into the offseason to make ends meet."

Said Dan Coughlin, "Willis was one hell of a player."

BOB GOLIC

Bob Golic has always been an emotional guy.

"It was just incredible putting that Browns uniform on and playing in that old stadium," he said. "I mean, I had gone to Browns games there with my dad. He also would take me to training camp at Hiram College quite a bit. I'd stand there with my little book and just ask people for autographs. I didn't even know if some of the guys who were signing the book were players or groundskeepers! I had no idea. But I didn't care. It was just really, really cool. I also had all the football cards as a kid. Bill Nelsen, Frank Ryan I loved. Gary Collins, Bill Glass, Jim Houston. When I was in CYO in grade school, one year Milt Morin came to speak at our awards dinner at the Brown Derby in Willowick [where Golic was raised]. I'll never forget that. It was very exciting."

Regarding his switch from linebacker to nose guard, Golic remembered getting a phone call from Bill Davis, the Browns' vice president of player personnel at the time. "He said, 'How do you feel about playing nose tackle?'" recalled Golic. "I basically told him, 'I don't really play nose tackle. I played there a little in college, but I'm more of a linebacker.' He said, 'Well, we claimed you off of waivers,' and I said, 'Oh yeah, I love nose tackle! Would love to do it!'"

It was difficult for Golic to change positions at first.

"It had been years since I'd even put my hands down in the dirt," he said. "And even when I did play nose tackle at Notre Dame, it was few and far between. So I just tried to develop myself into a position I didn't know much about."

Golic's first game as a Brown was in Los Angeles against the Raiders in the final preseason game of 1982. "I just remember seeing guys across the line," he laughed, "like Gene Upshaw, Dave Dalby, and Henry Lawrence—these big, massive people—and thinking, 'Man, this is gonna be a lot of work!'"

Later in that 1982 season, Golic became more comfortable at his new position. "I finally found a place to line up," he said. "I was learning the defenses and trying to understand. And I was actually starting to put on some weight because I came in as about a 245-pound linebacker."

By the late 1980s, Golic stood at 6-foot-3, 275 pounds and had mastered his position. "I found a way to be comfortable doing it," he said. "I knew where I had to get and found out how I was most comfortable getting there. I hustled, ran, did whatever I could. I think sometimes, even if you're halfway talented, as long as you love what you're doing and you really commit yourself to it, you're going to do pretty well."

"I told Coach [Sam] Rutigliano, 'That guy's really good. He's going to be a really quick nose tackle with a lot of power or he's going to be an average linebacker,'" said Joe DeLamielleure. "And he *was* a great nose tackle. He was tough. He had a lot of pride because he's from Cleveland. He was a great addition to the team."

"Bob was good at that nose tackle spot," said Mike Pruitt. "You couldn't move him. He wasn't that tall, but he did a great job."

"Golic was just a grind-it-out guy," Mike McLain added. "He gave it his all. You could see his love for the sport and his love for Cleveland."

"Bob put some blood and guts into the middle of that defensive line under Sam and into the Marty [Schottenheimer] years," said Ray Yannucci.

"You talk about playing with pain," said Jeff Schudel. "He left everything out on the field, everything. He just played hard every play. He was so sore after every game because of the way he played that he could barely drag himself to his car."

AND THE WINNER IS . . .
Bill Willis was as good as it gets when it comes to nose tackles. He simply dominated opposing centers. There was no one faster than him at getting to the quarterback.

Bob Golic was big and strong. Getting him out of the way was like trying to move a block of granite. And he knew how to perfect the position of nose tackle. He was sensational.

Bill Willis gets the nod when it comes to best Browns nose tackle of all time.

NOSE TACKLES WHO DID NOT MAKE THE CUT
No one knew who **Ahtyba Rubin** was when he got to the Browns. Nobody knew anything about him.

"He was just a guy, and there wasn't anything special about his build," said Steve King. "But when you saw the guy play, he could really play. He was really a very, very good player. Of all the players the Browns had during that era who weren't very good, Ahtyba Rubin was this guy who just came out of nowhere and became a very good player. He had a nice career with the Browns. You root for guys like that."

"That guy hustled his tail off," said Doug Dieken. "You'd see him at the sidelines making tackles. I liked the way he played. He was a good, solid player."

LINEBACKERS

The Candidates

Walt Michaels
Galen Fiss
Jim Houston
Clay Matthews
Chip Banks

Walt Michaels played mostly right linebacker for the Browns from 1952 to 1961. He totaled 11 interceptions in his career with a high of four in 1952. He returned two picks for touchdowns—a 34-yarder in 1953 and a 25-yarder in 1955. He was a Pro Bowler from 1955 to 1959.

Galen Fiss was mainly a left linebacker for the Browns from 1956 to 1966. He amassed 13 career interceptions with a high of four in 1962. He was a key cog to Browns teams that advanced to NFL championship games in 1964 and 1965, the former of which it won. He was picked for the Pro Bowl in 1962 and 1963.

Playing mostly middle linebacker for Cleveland from 1957 to 1966, Vince Costello never made any Pro Bowls, but he was as solid as they come. He had 22 career interceptions with a high of seven in 1963. He returned two fumbles for touchdowns—a 30-yarder in a 38–17 victory over Dallas on December 3, 1961, and a 21-yarder in a 41–14 rout of Pittsburgh on October 28, 1962.

Jim Houston began his NFL career at left defensive end but was switched to left linebacker early in his career, which

Jim Houston trying to take down Oilers quarterback Dan Pastorini in 1972 (PAUL TEPLEY/CLEVELAND STATE UNIVERSITY CLEVELAND PRESS ARCHIVES)

lasted from 1960 to 1972. He totaled 14 interceptions in his career with a high of three in both 1967 and 1968. He returned three picks for touchdowns. The first was a 42-yarder in a 38–24 victory over the Eagles on November 29, 1964. The second and third came in consecutive weeks—a 79-yarder in a 24–14 win over the Giants on December 3, 1967, and an 18-yarder in a 20–16 triumph over the Cardinals on December 10, 1967. He had 29.5 career sacks with a high of 8.5 in 1961. He was picked for the Pro Bowl in 1964, 1965, 1969, and 1970.

Charlie Hall played mostly left linebacker for the Browns from 1971 to 1980. He had 13 career interceptions with a high of three in 1974. That year, on October 6, he returned an interception 29 yards for a touchdown in a 40–24 loss to Oakland. In the season opener the next year, on September 21 in a 24–17 loss to the Bengals, he recovered a fumble in the end zone for a touchdown.

Dick Ambrose was mostly a middle linebacker for Cleveland from 1975 to 1983. He also played right inside linebacker and left inside linebacker. He had five career interceptions.

Manning mainly right outside linebacker for the Browns from 1978 to 1993, Clay Matthews had 16 career interceptions with a high of three in 1987, including a 26-yard pick-six in a 34–10 victory over Pittsburgh on September 20. He intercepted Jim Kelly at his own 1 yard line with three seconds left to preserve the Browns' 34–30 victory over the visiting Bills in an AFC divisional playoff on January 6, 1990. He returned a fumble 3 yards for the Browns' first score in a 51–0 rout of the Steelers on September 10, 1989. He recorded 82.5 career sacks with a high of 12 in 1984. Matthews was picked for the Pro Bowl in 1985 and from 1987 to 1989.

Chip Banks played left outside linebacker for the Browns from 1982 to 1986. He recorded five career interceptions with Cleveland with a high of three in 1983, including a 65-yard pick-six in a 30–0 defeat of New England on November 20. He totaled 27.5 sacks as a Brown with a high of 11 in 1985. He was First-Team All-Pro in 1983 and a Pro Bowler in 1982, 1983, 1985, and 1986.

Mike Johnson played mostly middle linebacker for the Browns from 1986 to 1993. He had 10 career interceptions as a Brown with a high of three in 1989. He returned an interception 64 yards for a touchdown in a 24–14 loss to the Chargers on September 23, 1990. He recovered a fumble in the end zone for a touchdown in a 37–21 win over Cincinnati on December 6, 1992. He totaled 11 career sacks with Cleveland with a high of four in 1993. He was picked for the Pro Bowl in 1989 and 1990.

The players in the running for best linebackers in Browns history are Michaels, Fiss, Houston, Matthews, and Banks.

Walt Michaels

Walt Michaels very possibly could have been a Hall of Famer. He just had a great career. He was a mainstay at linebacker.

"Michaels was smart, cerebral, understood the game. He was unbelievable and solid," said Steve King. "Every game, you got the best from Walt Michaels. You could make a case for him being the best linebacker the Browns have ever had because he did it for a long time. You knew you were always going to get great play from him. He was a gentleman, too. You don't have to worry about whether he's doing the right thing on Saturday night before a game. He's getting his sleep, he's doing the right thing, he's getting ready for the game."

Galen Fiss

Galen Fiss was the Browns' defensive leader and a guy who carried out the details of his assignments.

"A lot of times, the strong safety and the strong side line-backer have to work together," said Ross Fichtner, a Browns safety from 1960 to 1967. "One of the two was responsible for the run force on the strong side, so we had to coordinate via the defense with whatever defense was called. You could count on Galen doing his job all the time. And when someone does their job, it makes everybody else's job easier."

Jim Houston recalled Fiss as not only an outstanding line-backer but versatile, too. "When I moved to left linebacker, Galen switched to right linebacker with ease," he said. "That just gave you an idea of his capability, or his ability. Having been a left defensive end, I couldn't play right defensive end. Well, I could, but I'd certainly be weaker on the right side than I was on the left side."

"Galen was the rock," said Larry Benz, who played safety for the Browns from 1963 to 1965. "He had speed and size and could stop anybody. He was such a big hitter and was a devastating tackler. Running backs feared him."

Fiss was always in the middle of a play, close to the ball. "He was an excellent football player," Bill Glass said.

"He was getting up there in age in the mid-'60s," said Mike Peticca, "but you didn't think of him like that because he made so many plays and was a sturdy tackler. He could get out on the perimeter and chase down a guy running the sweep or be adept at pass coverage, guys coming out of the backfield. He was a very smart player."

Fiss was able to kid and tease and have fun with players but not ever in a way that would be hurtful. "There were certain players who were funny," Glass said, "but they were a little detrimental with their humor, whereas Galen was never that way. He always gave respect to everybody."

"Galen was a good leader," added Walter Roberts, a Browns kick returner from 1964 to 1966. "Some guys just exemplify that by their basic character, the way they're not quick to speak unless they really have something legitimate to say, just by trying to be fair and just. And that was Galen. There was a lot of integrity with him."

JIM HOUSTON

Paul Warfield compared Jim Houston with Jerry Sherk. That is high praise.

"It was not all power with Jim, but he certainly had that," said Warfield. "He had running speed, he had explosiveness off the ball, he came from a winning tradition at The Ohio State University. He truly fit in in terms of the Cleveland Browns' tradition. He was an outstanding player, a player who was unselfish. We always had players who were very high on the intellectual scale in terms of knowing what they were supposed to do and then having the discipline to get those things done. Jim Houston certainly epitomized that along with his great physical ability."

"He was a great player," Fred Hoaglin added. "He was quick and fast and strong at the point of attack."

"Jim was very knowledgeable about the defenses we played," said Ben Davis. "He was a leader on and off the field."

"I remember feeling pretty good about the defense, knowing that Houston was out there," Mike Peticca said. "He had a penchant for making big plays. He seemed like a guy who just never made a mistake. He was an outstanding player. During his prime, he was one of the best outside linebackers in the league."

When he was nine years old, Houston sat in the end zone of old Cleveland Municipal Stadium and watched his older brother Lin play for the Browns.

"I just wondered what it would take to be on the field," he said. "And then to go to Massillon [Washington] and be a high school All-American, All-Ohio, and then be recruited by Woody Hayes and go to Columbus and have success there, and then get drafted by the Browns . . . to have all this come true . . . it was magic."

CLAY MATTHEWS

It didn't take long for Clay Matthews to adapt to playing right outside linebacker his rookie year with the Browns after having played on the inside for four years at USC.

"It took me a year or two to figure out what to do out there. There was a lot more space," he said in the summer 2005 *Bernie's Insiders.* "I think I got the hang of it eventually."

That is the Understatement of the Century.

After injuring his knee during the 1978 training camp, Matthews eventually replaced Gerald Irons midway through that season. "It [right outside linebacker] ended up being a great place to play," he continued in the summer 2005 *Bernie's Insiders.* "I wouldn't have traded it for anything."

Matthews always took it year by year.

"When you come into the league, at first you're just happy to be there," he said in the summer 2005 *Bernie's Insiders.* "Then all the talk from everyone when you get to years five and six, all of a sudden, you're an old player, an old man. The average NFL career is a little over three years. It develops a line of thinking that one of these days it's all going to end. I honestly went from years five and six to 15 thinking, 'Well, next year, it'll all be gone.' Then I'd come back to training camp, and after one day I'd always call my wife and say, 'I've still got it.' She'd always laugh. The buildup to training camp is an emotional buildup. All year, you've been hearing you're old. When you go in there, there is some degree of worry about whether your skills will still be good. But usually after one practice, you'd realize you could still do some things."

Clay Matthews in action against the Seahawks on November 11, 1979
(PAUL TEPLEY/CLEVELAND STATE UNIVERSITY CLEVELAND PRESS ARCHIVES)

Matthews was year in, year out simply a very, very good player. He seldom missed tackles, he was very good at covering players coming out of the backfield, and he was an excellent pass-rusher. "He was a great athlete, and I think that is shown by how so many from his family overall have really achieved in the NFL," said Mike Peticca. "He wasn't real flashy, he just played, and he played so well. He made lots of big plays. It was a real luxury, I think even among the players, to just know that Clay Matthews was there. He was very smart and helped keep the team loose with his personality. I wish he was in the Hall of Fame. He was never Lawrence Taylor, but he was so, so good for so long. He was the definition of dependability and excellence."

"Clay was a model on endurance," said Mike McLain. "He was probably the first great pass rusher the Browns had since Bill Glass. He could make plays all over the field."

"For his position, Clay was the best player I ever played with and played against, and that's saying a lot," Joe DeLamielleure said. "He was the toughest guy to block because he was so quick. He was amazing, and he could cover. He should be in the Hall of Fame."

"Why this guy is not in the Hall of Fame I don't know," said Doug Dieken. "He had the quickest feet. His feet were unbelievable. You never saw him off his feet. The coaches used him a lot in coverage because he could run with the tight ends, so he didn't get the big sack totals that he could've gotten if they'd let him rush every time."

"He arguably should be in the Pro Football Hall of Fame," said Ray Yannucci. "I think what keeps him out of the Hall is that he wasn't a dominating force like, say, a Lawrence Taylor, somebody of that ilk, during that time. But he was a tremendous football player, a hell of a linebacker. He could cover and he could stop the run. And his longevity speaks for itself."

CHIP BANKS

Unfortunately, off-the-field problems likely cost Chip Banks a bronze bust in the Pro Football Hall of Fame.

"I don't ever remember seeing a linebacker that big," said Mike McLain. "Until offensive lineman Keith Bosley, who was a strike-replacement player in 1987, I was told Banks was issued the biggest set of shoulder pads in team history. He had loads of talent. He could've been clearly a Hall of Famer. It's sad what happened to him."

Banks's talent, his God-given ability, was obvious. It is a real shame because he had everything from a physical standpoint to be one of the all-time greats. "What more can you say about his physical abilities, his speed, his strength?" asked Mike Peticca. "And I think he was a very smart player, but things got in the way. He never figured it out."

"Banks probably had more physical talent than any Browns player that I covered, but he never took advantage of it," Ray Yannucci added.

"Chip had amazing talent," said Doug Dieken. "If he'd wanted it, he could've been one of the best who ever played, but he just didn't always channel his energy in the right directions. The guy was freakish athletically. We were indoors one day, and I saw him throw a football about 60 yards."

"He was so fast around that right side," said Jeff Schudel. "When he was on his game, he was so quick. He was so strong naturally, he never had to work out. His body just looked like a sculpture."

"Had he remained in Cleveland, he'd be the best linebacker the Browns have ever had," Steve King said. "He made the Pro Bowl four years with the Browns, and he only played for them for five years. I remember CBS Radio was doing the Browns' Thursday night game with the Bengals in 1983. Jack Buck was the play-by-play guy, and Hank Stram was the color guy. Stram had gone into the locker room to talk to Banks, and he just raved about what a physical specimen he was. He said, 'He looked like Superman with his shirt off.' Banks could do it all. Think about this. If Banks had not messed up and zoned out and been dedicated to playing and had Don Rogers [a Browns free safety in 1984 and 1985 who died of a drug overdose] lived, those two guys would probably be in the Hall of Fame and the Browns would've won a Super Bowl or two or three."

AND THE WINNERS ARE . . .

It really is a shame that **Clay Matthews** is not in the Pro Football Hall of Fame. He is so deserving of that honor. He played 16 seasons with the Browns and three more with the Falcons. He got better as the years went on. He definitely notches one spot as one of the best linebackers in Browns history.

Walt Michaels is another player who should perhaps be in the Hall of Fame. He didn't play as long as Matthews did, but he still had a pretty darned long NFL career. He gets another spot as one of Cleveland's greatest linebackers ever.

Jim Houston also had a lengthy career in the NFL. You typically do not hear his name and the Hall of Fame in the same breath, but that certainly does not mean that he didn't have an outstanding career. He garners the final spot as one of the team's best linebackers in history.

LINEBACKERS WHO DID NOT MAKE THE CUT

Vince Costello epitomized what the Cleveland Browns were about.

"Vince was a guy who was one of those excellent leaders," said Paul Warfield. "He and Galen Fiss were the players who had been around for quite some time. We had players who had the physical ability to play professional football at the highest level in a physical sense, but we had football players who, knowing what you were to do and having the discipline to execute it—not once every three or four plays but *every* play—were the essence of the team. Vince and Galen were a part of the leadership on the team. They were the captains. They were able to diffuse that into the other players because that's what the Cleveland Browns were about, and winning was of the essence."

"Vince was probably one of the most knowledgeable guys I ever played with," Jim Kanicki said. "He was a team leader and knew what everyone around him should be doing."

Costello was a guy who was always thought of as very reliable. "Vince was a good middle linebacker," said Jim Ray Smith.

"Without the [1964] championship, my career kind of would've been a nothing, there would have been something missing," Costello said. "That kind of fulfilled all the highlights that you want."

Charlie Hall was one of those players who may not have had a great aspect to his game, but he was good in every category. He was not necessarily a Pro Bowl caliber player year in, year out, but he was above average. He was too good for other teams to potentially attack. He was really solid and dependable, hardly ever missed games. "He was in that in-between era when the Browns were often competitive but not great," said Mike Peticca. "I think that his record of being out there for every game for a long time tells you all you need to know that he was a good, good player."

"Hall, who was on defenses that really weren't that good, was an outstanding player," Steve King said. "He played the run, he played the pass, he always knew where he was supposed to be. Had he been with the Steelers, the Cowboys, the Vikings, or some of the other great teams of the '70s, that guy would've been going to the Pro Bowl every year. He was a very good player. He had the abilities to make plays. He never, ever wanted to draw the attention to himself. He wasn't about individualism, he was

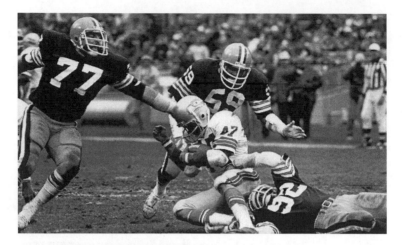

Charlie Hall (59) defends against Seattle's Sherman Smith on November 11, 1979 (PAUL TEPLEY/CLEVELAND STATE UNIVERSITY CLEVELAND PRESS ARCHIVES)

about the team. Especially in the 1980 season, he made some big, big stops. He was a key guy in that drive to the AFC Central championship. He may have saved the best for last when it came to his career."

"Charlie was a good linebacker," said Mike Pruitt. "He was consistent, which is what you want."

When **Dick Ambrose** got drafted by the Browns, the only thing he really knew about Cleveland was the Browns.

"I grew up in New Rochelle, New York, which is a suburb of New York City, and the Browns and Giants used to play at least twice every year," he said. "I'd go watch them play one another at Yankee Stadium, so the Browns were a team I was familiar with. I became much *more* familiar when I got to Cleveland about the depth of the tradition and the community's love for the team."

Ambrose's first week of training camp with the Browns' other rookies was definitely an experience he will never forget.

"None like I ever had before," he said in the March 2005 *Bernie's Insiders.* "Everybody was bigger. No issue there. It did seem like an uphill battle, though. It was almost like a constant scrimmage every practice. It was almost a full-go contact session. By the end of the week, I had gotten comfortable with the fact that, yeah, I thought I belonged here and was able to assess myself based on what I saw from the other guys and thought I might have a good chance [of making the team]."

Then the veterans reported.

"It was oh my gosh, these guys are enormous and it was two or three classes up from where we were as rookies," Ambrose said in the March 2005 *Bernie's Insiders.* "It was like taking five steps backward. It was very easy to get down on yourself and get dejected because of the numbers game that exists every year in training camp."

Ambrose, though, knew he had what it took to play in the NFL. "There's no sense in doing something half-speed," he continued in the March 2005 *Bernie's Insiders.* "I go all out all the time or at least as much as possible. I don't really believe in absolutes. That was my attitude even when I was running into a guy twice my size and it was probably going to hurt. But I knew I was going to hurt a lot more if I didn't go all out. I realized I could knock those guys [veterans] down, I could tackle those guys, I could avoid blocks. I enjoyed it. I loved to play the game and liked what I did. I liked trying to be the best at what I was doing. There were dog days, of course, but every day was kind of a new challenging experience. I even looked forward to practices and enjoyed them."

Ambrose's adjustment from college to the pros was not exactly smooth sailing, but playing behind the likes of Jerry Sherk and Walter Jonson helped big time. "That was quite an impression," he said. "I certainly looked up to those guys."

"Dick was one of those guys who was tough right there in the middle," said Pruitt. "That's probably one of the toughest positions to play, middle linebacker, because everybody is coming at you from all different directions. You have linemen coming at you, you have running backs coming at you, you have the center coming at you. You have to fend off all these people and still try to make a tackle. Dick did a good job for us."

"When I was in Buffalo, [head coach] Lou Saban loved Dick," said Joe DeLamielleure. "Every time we watched him practice, he'd say, 'We're gonna get that guy, we're gonna try to trade for him. We've got to get him on our team. He's not big, he's not fast, but the guy is around the ball all the time. He's always around the ball.' I respected Dick. When I got to Cleveland, I felt, 'Man, if I can block Dick Ambrose consistently in practice, I'll be a pretty good player.'"

"In coming back to the organization in '76 and '77, if I noticed a change, players like Galen Fiss, Vince Costello, and Jim Houston, there were not many of those players around, but Dick Ambrose, on the other hand, epitomized that in my mind," Warfield said. "Not only was he a little bit undersized as a middle linebacker, but he had the toughness to play the football and certainly had the intellect that was part of the Cleveland Browns organization."

The switch from 4-3 to 3-4 on defense in 1980 under new defensive coordinator Marty Schottenheimer took some adjusting for Ambrose, who was positioned at right inside linebacker, where he stayed for the most part the rest of his career.

"I soon got the hang of it," he said. "Because you're not shielded as much [in the 3-4], you're facing a guard usually, the keys are a little bit different. I think it was overall good in retrospect only because we probably were a little stronger at linebacker than we were at defensive line back then, so we put the emphasis on a more mobile defense and one that didn't rely so much on defensive linemen to rush the passer. It got the line-backers more involved, and that actually turned out to be one of the strong points of Clay Matthews and Robert L. Jackson, who could both rush the passer very well, so that helped."

"Dick wasn't a high draft pick," said Doug Dieken, "but if you had to block him you said, 'We-e-e-l-l-l, let me think about this one.' He was going to hit you before you hit him."

"He was hardnosed and smart," Mike McLain said. "He was one of those guys you need in the middle of your defense."

Mike Johnson was a tackling machine.

"A lot of guys will say, 'Well, Mike Johnson made the tackle several yards downfield.' Okay, whatever, but he made the tackle," said King. "He played with a lot of heart. He was a very good athlete and had a nose for the ball. He and Clay Matthews . . . were they the best pair of linebackers the Browns have ever had? I don't know, but they certainly have to be in the running. Johnson didn't need to be told twice what to do."

Johnson was known for his strength and hard hitting. He was a borderline star. He was one reason the linebacking unit in the late 1980s and early 1990s was good. "He might've typi-fied that group of linebackers that they were overall really good units," said Peticca. "He was one of those guys who you knew you had who was above average, a good player."

"He was a very good run defender," Jeff Schudel said. "He had good anticipation of where a play was going. He could see it developing before it did, and that made it hard for teams to block him."

CORNERBACKS

Warren Lahr
Don Paul
Bernie Parrish
Hanford Dixon
Frank Minnifield

Tommy James played right cornerback and also right safety for the Browns from 1948 to 1955. He was a vital part of some fine Browns defenses that helped the team to several championships. He had 34 career interceptions with a high of nine in 1950. He returned an interception 27 yards for a touchdown in a 14–3 win over the New York Yankees on September 18, 1949. He returned a fumble 37 yards for a touchdown in a 27–16 victory over the Chicago Cardinals on November 29, 1953. That season, he was picked for his only Pro Bowl.

Playing mostly left cornerback for the Browns from 1949 to 1959, Warren Lahr had 44 career interceptions, five of which he returned for touchdowns. He had two pick-sixes in 1950 in consecutive weeks—a 30-yarder in a 13–7 victory over Philadelphia on December 3 and an 18-yarder in a 45–21 win over Washington on December 10. He returned two interceptions for touchdowns in 1951—a 23-yarder in a 38–23 triumph over the Rams on October 7 and a 27-yarder in a 17–0 victory over the Steelers on October 21. He had another 27-yard pick-six in a 39–10 win over the Bears on November 14, 1954. Lahr was a Pro Bowler in 1953.

A right cornerback for Cleveland from 1954 to 1958, Don Paul totaled 22 career interceptions with the Browns. He returned an interception 35 yards for a touchdown in a 24–16 loss to the Steelers on October 28, 1956. He had a 65-yard pick-six in a 38–14 victory over the Los Angeles Rams in the NFL championship game on December 26, 1955. He returned a fumble 89 yards for a touchdown in a 24–0 win over Pittsburgh on November 10, 1957. Paul was a Pro Bowler from 1956 to 1958.

Bernie Parrish was a left cornerback for the Browns from 1959 to 1966. He amassed 29 career interceptions for Cleveland with a high of seven in 1961. He returned three picks for touchdowns. He returned an interception 37 yards for a touchdown in a 17–7 win over the Cardinals on October 18, 1959. He had a 92-yard pick-six in a 42–0 victory over the Bears on December 11, 1960. He returned an interception 54 yards for the winning score in a 20–16 victory over Dallas on October 18, 1964. He returned a fumble 34 yards for a touchdown in a 38–17 triumph over the Cowboys on December 3, 1961. Parrish was a Pro Bowler in 1960 and 1963.

Manning mostly the left cornerback position for Cleveland from 1965 to 1971, Erich Barnes totaled 18 career interceptions for the Browns, including three returned for touchdowns. He returned an interception 40 yards for a touchdown in a 24–21 victory over the Redskins on December 8, 1968. He had a 55-yard pick-six in a 42–31 win over Pittsburgh on October 18, 1969. He returned an interception 38 yards for a touchdown in a 15–7 victory over the Steelers on October 3, 1970. He was a Pro Bowler in 1968.

The solid and steady Ben Davis played right cornerback for Cleveland from 1967 to 1973, amassing 17 career interceptions with the Browns with a high of eight in 1968.

Clarence Scott was mostly a left cornerback for Cleveland from 1971 to 1983. He had 39 career interceptions with a high of five in 1973. That year, on September 16, he returned an interception 45 yards for a touchdown in a 24–14 win over Baltimore. He had a 49-yard pick-six in a 24–23 win over the Oilers on October 16, 1977. He was picked for the Pro Bowl in 1973.

Playing right cornerback for the Browns from 1981 to 1989, Hanford Dixon had 26 career interceptions with a high of five in both 1984 and 1986. He picked off Terry Bradshaw three times to help the Browns to a crucial 10–9 victory over the Steelers on December 19, 1982. He was First-Team All-Pro in 1986 and 1987 and a Pro Bowler from 1986 to 1988.

A Browns left cornerback from 1984 to 1992, Frank Minnifield had 20 career interceptions with a high of four in both 1987 and 1988. He returned an interception 48 yards for a touchdown that sealed a 38–21 victory over Indianapolis in an AFC divisional playoff on January 9, 1988. He was First-Team All-Pro in 1988 and a Pro Bowler from 1986 to 1989.

Anthony Henry played mostly left cornerback for Cleveland from 2001 to 2004. He totaled 17 career interceptions for the Browns with a high of—and a league-leading—10 his rookie year. He returned an interception 97 yards for a touchdown in a 15–10 defeat to the Jaguars on December 16, 2001.

Manning left cornerback from 2010 to 2016, Joe Haden amassed 19 career interceptions for Cleveland with a high of six in his rookie year of 2010. He returned an interception 29 yards for a touchdown in a 41–20 loss to the Bengals on November 17, 2013. He was picked for the Pro Bowl in 2013 and 2014.

The players in the running for best cornerbacks in Browns history are Lahr, Paul, Parrish, Dixon, and Minnifield.

WARREN LAHR

Warren Lahr was simply a great cornerback.

"You look at what Lahr did, and he's second in career interceptions in team history, one behind [safety] Thom Darden," said Steve King. "You've got to remember, the Browns back in Lahr's day were playing against the Detroit Lions and Bobby Layne and the Los Angeles Rams with Bob Waterfield and Norm Van Brocklin. Those were prolific passing attacks. Lahr was one of the cornerstones of those Browns' defensive backfields. There wasn't a better defensive backfield in the NFL."

"Warren was a real good player, was smart, was a good tackler, and was good in zone coverage," John Wooten said.

DON PAUL

Don Paul was a big-play guy.

"His interception return for a score in the 1955 championship game got the Browns off and running out in Los Angeles," said Steve King. "A lot of people don't remember him. He wasn't flashy, but he was solid, very good. You don't play a long time like that in Paul Brown's defensive backfield unless you're pretty good."

"Don was a pretty good player," Dan Coughlin said.

BERNIE PARRISH

Bernie Parrish was a game-film guru who called the defensive signals.

"I just had a knack, or an ability, to be able to do that," he said. "Lots of folks can look at the films, but they don't know what the hell they're looking at. That just happened to be something I was good at, and it helped our strategy among our players."

"Parrish really knew the game of football and really did his homework game after game," said Tom Melody.

"He was definitely a student of the game," added Walter Beach.

Paul Warfield had a great appreciation for Parrish. "Bernie had fine ability, but in terms of studying, I gained a great appreciation for that," he said. "He sort of 'adopted' me to a certain extent, so that mental aspect plays a great role in the success of professional football players. Bernie showed me the things that he would do in terms of study of wide receivers and how he used the philosophies of the Cleveland Browns. So when he had to be in certain situations and go against wide receivers such as Tommy McDonald, he knew precisely what they would attempt to do in terms of having success. It was very helpful for me in terms of my understanding and relating later on to specific cornerbacks who I had to work with. But it was more than that, beyond that. I had to also learn who the defensive coordinators were, what their philosophies were, how they tried to stop me, and the things that I liked to do. And then my game had to evolve. So the essence of the Cleveland Browns—and I'm talking about players like Bernie Parrish, Galen Fiss, and Vince Costello—emanated from Paul Brown on to Blanton Collier. That was the intellectual side of football and how important that was, enabling one to have success even in a team setting."

"Bernie was like a coach on the field for the defensive backs," said Jim Kanicki.

Parrish believes the Browns had little chance of upsetting the Baltimore Colts in the 1964 NFL championship game had he not called the defensive signals.

"Hell no," he said. "We sure as hell wouldn't have shut them out."

The way Parrish and Walter Beach covered Raymond Berry and Jimmy Orr in that game was amazing. "The Colts' passing routes were so precise during the regular season," said Mike Peticca, "and I guess it was Parrish who came up with the idea, 'Well, let's disrupt that precision by taking them on basically right off the line of scrimmage.' I don't think anyone used the words 'bump-and-run' then, but the way Parrish and Beach covered Berry and Orr was essentially that. You can even see in game films almost just by watching John Unitas where it looks like he's ready to throw, but the Browns' pass rush is all over him. It would probably be risky to say the Browns' defense never played that way again until years later, but probably in that era they never played it as extensively as in that '64 title game."

For some reason, the Browns' coaches did not want Parrish to call the defensive signals in the following season's league title game in Green Bay. "Blanton told me that if I called my own defensive signals, Art Modell was going to have me removed from the stadium by NFL security," said Parrish. "Now, Art Modell never confirmed that, so Blanton could've been using it just to keep control of the god damned signals. We got our asses beat because I didn't get to call my game. I called the games most of the time that year, but more and more the coaches wanted to assert their own control over it. They had their own game plan, and it was stupid, it was the dumbest game plan I've ever seen. It cost us the god damned football game. We'd have beaten the Packers if they'd let me call my god damned signals. They *didn't* let me call the defensive signals against the Colts the year before. They called the defenses from the sideline, and I simply ignored them. I called whatever I wanted to. And Coach [Nick] Skorich would not cross me, and Skorich told me at halftime when we had [the Colts] shut out, 'Just keep doing what you're doing.'"

"Bernie was a great player for his size," Bobby Franklin, mainly a Browns right safety from 1960 to 1966, said. "He was tough and a take-charge type of guy. He had average speed, but his intelligence made up for it."

"I had a terrific experience with the Browns," said Parrish. "My teammates were great people, wonderful people. That was probably the greatest experience of my life. And the Browns' fans have got to be the best fans in the world to play for. They were wonderful. They were the greatest, most appreciative people. I couldn't have had a better career or a better life. That was the greatest eight years a guy could have. I had a great time. I loved it there in Cleveland."

HANFORD DIXON

Hanford Dixon was, hands down, one of the best defensive backs the Browns have ever had.

"Hanford was quick, he knew what to do, he was right there, he could run step for step with some of the best receivers in the game," said Mike Pruitt.

"He, in my opinion, should be in the Hall of Fame," Joe DeLamielleure said. "He was a shut-down corner, physical, he tackled. He was a unique player."

Dixon had a rough rookie season in 1981. His coming-out party was his three-interception game against the Steelers in 1982, which helped the Browns qualify for the playoffs.

"Dixon, for a short guy, was one of the top corners in the league," said Mike McLain. "It was great use of a first-round pick."

FRANK MINNIFIELD

Frank Minnifield claims he was the first NFL player to take a laptop computer into the classroom.

"And that was before laptops were commonplace for everybody," he said. "There were a whole lot of things that I wanted to keep track of about the wide receivers I covered. I wanted to keep track of the way they blocked, how they lined up, how they used the width of the field, the things they did when they were going to run, the things they did when they were going to pass . . . and I couldn't do that with a pencil and paper."

Minnifield said his studious approach to the game stemmed from playing under coaching legend George Allen for two years in the United States Football League. "Coach Allen gave me homework to do on all the receivers who I was going to play against," said Minnifield, who was a walk-on at the University of Louisville. "And I had to give him a report on those receivers."

Minnifield's tough road to the NFL in which he was never handed anything on a silver platter was a big reason for his success.

"I think the fact that I really had to try to outwork everybody all the way from high school to the pros," he said, "lent itself to a mental state that was willing to work hard all the time. There weren't any of these things where you knew there was a coach who liked you and that he was going to play you no matter how bad you played. Nobody made any promises to me anywhere down the line. The only promise they made was they'd let me try."

Another crucial factor that resulted in Minnifield's success in the NFL was the rules changes that had occurred in the late 1970s, which were supposed to favor the offense. Those rules changes, ironically, were what actually presented him the opportunity to *play* in the NFL. "In the '70s," he explained, "the game was to knock wide receivers off their feet and not let them run through zones. I wasn't big enough to knock people down. I mean, I'm not going to knock big Harold Carmichael down or James Lofton. I'm not going to knock them off their feet. So you put me in the '70s, and I'm cut in training camp."

Finally, Minnifield's stature and physical skills—namely his speed, quickness, and incredible jumping ability—added up to essentially what NFL teams were looking for at the time.

"The big, tall, rangy cornerback was a dinosaur at this point," he said, "because all the wide receivers were now smaller guys like the 'Marks Brothers' in Miami, the 'Three Amigos' out in Denver, the 'Smurfs' in Washington . . . you didn't have to be real big to play these guys. They were going to try to beat you at the line of scrimmage and go deep. You had to be so quick at the line of scrimmage. So all the things that I could do well became extremely valuable to defenses during those years. What I could do well was, you couldn't go around me. That was what I could do as well as anybody in the league or better. I wanted to line up on the receiver at the line of scrimmage and keep him there until the play was over."

There weren't too many players who could play man-to-man like Minnifield could. "I don't care how big the receivers were, Frank would go right up to them and go one-on-one with them, step for step," Mike Pruitt said. "He wasn't a big guy, but he was probably at that time one of the best defensive backs around."

"That guy was unreal," said Joe DeLamielleure. "He could jump out of the gym. He was physical and could tackle."

"He was a borderline great cornerback when he was at his best," Mike McLain said.

When Minnifield joined the Browns, a strong defense was being built. "'Minnie' was the final piece to the puzzle," said Hanford Dixon. "You know how sometimes you have something and you just need one more thing to complete it? Well, Minnifield was it. 'Minnie' and I just clicked. There were no two corners better prepared for each game than the two of us. We studied film at home, and we knew everything about the wide receivers we covered—their moves, how many steps they took ... hell, we knew when they went to the bathroom and how long they were in there!"

Dixon was bigger than Minnifield. "Hanford's height, arm's length, weight, his size in general, afforded him the opportunity to play the game differently than me," said Minnifield. "The players who gave me trouble, he handled easy. The players who gave him trouble, I handled easy."

Dixon's size advantage meant he covered the bigger wide receivers. "The coaches let us decide," he said. "We knew exactly what we were going to do and how we were going to cover the receivers. We didn't even go to the huddle, we just went to our positions."

Many cornerbacks played bump-and-run at the time, but the Browns' dynamic duo perfected the scheme with a different twist. "A lot of cornerbacks would start to run before they got the jam," explained Dixon. "We stayed in the jam because we knew if we missed the jam, we were fast enough that we'd catch up."

"I called them chipmunks. They used to chatter like chipmunks," laughed Ray Yannucci. "The Browns didn't have what I say was a big-time defense until they brought in Minnifield and Dixon. They became the cornerstones of that backfield for several years. They were probably two of the finest cornerbacks the Browns have ever had."

"Those guys really took pride in the way they played," Jeff Schudel said. "Hanford relied on his natural abilities to cover, and Minnifield was a student of the game."

"They were the triggermen for the fun that was the Browns of the late '80s," said Steve King. "Those two guys identified with the fans better than in any sport at any time. They were Pro Bowl corners, they were the two best corners in the league.

A lot of teams didn't even go to Dixon's or Minnifield's sides, so they tested the middle of the defensive backfield. That's why, had Don Rogers lived, a lot of things would've been different. With Rogers back there, you've got both corners covered, you've got the middle covered, where are you going to throw the football? Dixon and Minnifield were just unbelievable. I once asked Hanford, 'Do you ever think about The Drive game and those opportunities that kind of slipped away?' I saw a tear roll down his cheek. He said, 'Oh yeah, I think about it all the time. Those were games that really were opportunities lost.' If you think about it, if the Browns go to the Super Bowl once or maybe twice, and they have that exposure on the big stage and they get to play in front of the whole world, Dixon, Minnifield, and probably Clay Matthews are all in the Hall of Fame."

"Hanford and Minnifield were the best cornerback tandem ever maybe," said DeLamielleure.

Again, the film study at home plus regular film sessions with the team made the difference for both Minnifield and Dixon, who began using the same approach soon after Minnifield arrived in Cleveland. The two of them soon became known as the "Corner Brothers." The Browns' close loss to Miami in the 1985 divisional playoffs in which they held the vaunted Marks Brothers—receivers Mark Duper and Mark Clayton—to one reception between the two was the game that really vaulted Minnifield and Dixon to national prominence, according to Minnifield.

"I think that game really kind of propelled me and Hanford into a different level in the National Football League," he said. "That's the first time we did something that gave us notice nationwide."

"To be honest," said Dixon, "I think we were noticed before that. I guarantee you, Duper and Clayton knew what they were in for before that game."

"Hanford and I were kind of like the poster boys for a great defense in Cleveland," said Minnifield. "When we lost, we took a lot of criticism. When we won, we got a lot of credit. So we spent an inordinate amount of time trying to win football games."

Minnifield and Dixon were absolutely sensational at man-to-man coverage. "Hanford and I really felt like we had to dominate the game from start to finish whether it was a run or whether it was a pass," Minnifield said.

According to Minnifield, it was important for him and Dixon to be aware of not only the receivers they were covering but also the entire defensive scheme. "In order to know where you've got to help the defense and where the defense is vulnerable, you've got to know what everybody is doing," he said. "And you've got to be concerned about whether that player is going to do what he's supposed to do. So I looked at our safeties and linebackers as a support group for me and Hanford—and I'm not saying that in a derogatory way toward them. We would decide which receiver was the biggest threat to us, and we would give the safeties the okay to leave one corner without any protection."

Minnifield liked covering receivers on the outside, while Dixon favored covering them on the inside. "Players who ran across the field towards the middle of the field, Hanford would be in better position," he said. "Players who ran routes on the outside of the field, I would be in better position."

Both Minnifield and Dixon were extraordinarily confident. "I mean, even when they [receivers] beat us, we thought it was luck," Minnifield said. "We didn't think they beat us because they could beat us, they beat us because something happened that was lucky, something happened that gave them that opportunity. It wasn't because they lined up and just beat us."

Minnifield's most memorable interceptions came in victories over the Houston Oilers. "Intercepting Warren Moon three times in '87 down at the Astrodome and twice in overtime the year before in Cleveland," he said. "I'll never forget those two games."

According to Minnifield, the notion by many that the Browns went into a "prevent" defense on John Elway's 98-yard march in The Drive game is nothing more than a myth. "I thought it was aggressive play calling, I didn't think it was anywhere close to being a 'prevent,'" he said. "As a matter of fact, I don't even remember practicing 'prevents' in Cleveland during those years. We didn't have a defense that we called 'prevent.'"

Back in the mid- to late 1980s, you couldn't say "Minnifield" without saying "Dixon," and you couldn't say "Dixon" without saying "Minnifield." One went together with the other. And during training camp in 1984, the two of them created the original "dawg pound," which eventually the bleachers section of old Cleveland Stadium became, in order to liven things up a bit. They began barking—yes, barking—at the defensive linemen.

"We wanted to get them going," said Dixon. "We wanted them to be the dogs and to look at the quarterback as the cat. The whole thing was meant for the defensive line, but at Lakeland [Community College] the fans were so close to the playing field that they just took it over and took off with it. Everybody on a team needs something to identify with. That was the thing for us. This dawg thing was just right on time."

It coincided with the Browns' new winning ways starting the next season after a string of below-par seasons. And, boy, did it ever take off. Neither Minnifield nor Dixon had any idea that their woofing would be the start of, quite possibly, the largest, loudest, longest-running canine commotion this side of the motion picture *101 Dalmatians*. "It really wasn't anything planned with anybody trying to do anything," Minnifield remembered. "It just happened, and when it happened, there were a lot of people who latched on to it, and it took off."

During the next 10-plus seasons and on into today's more contrived version of the Dawg Pound, legions of Browns fans not only have barked their lungs out but also have attired themselves in dog masks, painted their faces, and even feasted on dog biscuits!

"I'm just so proud that people have associated my name with it for all these years. It is amazing," said Minnifield. "We're looking at almost 40 years of the Dawg Pound . . . it seemed like it was just yesterday that me and Hanford were giving high fives to all the guys in the dawg pound."

"Minnifield and Dixon were so, so good and so fun," Mike Peticca said. "I think that aspect of it—the dawg pound and all of that stuff—might sound like a really fun thing, but I think it was also a big benefit as far as creating an attitude. They were both such great cover corners. The sad thing about them is that they gave so much . . . the definition of their job, being on an island against all those great receivers not just week in and week out but virtually every play. I think that wore on them, and by the end of multiple seasons they were playing with bad hamstrings and they were still playing well, even if hobbled. They were both Hall of Fame talents. They didn't have the longevity of some guys. It's not fair that guys are penalized for not being on a Super Bowl winner. I don't know how you can overrate how excellent they were covering great receivers. And they were tough against the run, too. They were tough, tough guys, so physically gifted. And they were smart. They inspired the team, they inspired the whole fan base. When you talk about the all-time greats of the Browns franchise, each of them deserves to be included, and just think, they were out there together! That was amazing!"

"It's amazing," said Minnifield, "how many people still greet me as I'm passing through the airport on my way to the rail car and going throughout the city. I think probably the biggest compliment that most of these players pay to the Cleveland Browns is when they play for several teams—say, a guy played two years for the Browns, two years for Pittsburgh, two years for Seattle, something like that—they tell people they played for the Cleveland Browns. They list the Cleveland Browns as the team they played for when they have to list something. And I always find that amusing. Instead of listing all the teams, they list the Cleveland Browns. Once you're in the fraternity of the Cleveland Browns, you don't all of a sudden become somebody else. You're always a Cleveland Brown."

AND THE WINNERS ARE . . .

It was a difficult decision to leave Warren Lahr off of the list of the two greatest cornerbacks in Browns history. But **Hanford Dixon** and **Frank Minnifield** were such fine cornerbacks, they just had to be on the list—both of them. Again, you can't mention one without the other.

CORNERBACKS WHO DID NOT MAKE THE CUT

Tommy James was one of many players who made great contributions to the early days of the Browns' success.

"James was a great player, just a great corner," said Steve King. "When Paul Brown saw that James had lost a step or two, he moved him from corner to safety, and James did not like it at all. Brown did what he thought was best for the team, and James played very well at safety after he was moved. But he wanted to be a corner. That's like taking a strikeout pitcher and saying, 'Hey, we want you to throw off-speed pitches and get guys to hit the ball into the ground.'"

"Tommy was a very good player," said Dan Coughlin.

Erich Barnes had great physical ability and was a very punishing player, a tough player.

"Barnes was a great player, just an unbelievable player," King said. "He was a guy who was tough, and he didn't make any bones about it. He tackled from the neck up. He wasn't afraid to clothesline somebody, he wasn't afraid to go after somebody. He was going to punish receivers coming across the field. Nowadays, all of those would be penalties. He had a tremendous career with the Browns."

"Erich was a tough, hardnosed player, physical," said Fred Hoaglin. "People now don't play like he played. You just don't see corners hitting people like he did. He'd take out tight ends with a forearm. He was also one of the fastest guys in the NFL when he played."

"When he played for the Giants, we considered him a dirty player," laughed Dan Coughlin. "When he played for the Browns, he was considered just a highly competitive guy. He was good."

Ben Davis may have come farther than any Browns player in history.

"He came from tiny Defiance College. Defiance!" King said. "To come from there and to be a defensive back on great Browns teams in the late '60s, it was amazing. He wasn't the biggest guy but a guy who was able to position to make plays. He had great technique. A lot of times, he got the opposing team's best receiver, and he wasn't afraid of that. He was a guy who won a lot of battles."

"I worked against Ben every day in practice and had a great appreciation for his abilities as a cornerback," said Paul Warfield. "Had he not injured his knee, he could have become one of the outstanding cornerbacks in the National Football League. He came back from the injury and still was able to contribute at a high level."

"Ben was smart, a good coverage guy, could run well," John Wooten said.

Year in and year out, **Clarence Scott** was a great player.

"Clarence was smooth as silk," said Doug Dieken. "He was one of my favorite teammates. We were drafted together, and we had rookie camp at Case Western Reserve. People were booing Clarence because they thought the Browns should've drafted Jack Tatum. Obviously, the Ohio State faithful wanted Tatum, but I think Clarence had a much better career than Jack Tatum did."

"Scott was a pro's pro," said King. "He didn't let the struggles of the team during the '70s impede his progress. He was as good as it got, he was really one of the top corners in the AFC. He was that good. Had he been with the Steelers instead of the Browns, he would've been a guy who they'd have been talking about as a Hall of Famer. In '79, Sam Rutigliano moved him to safety. He didn't like it but never, ever said a word. Instead, he learned to be a pretty good safety."

Case in point, in 1980 the Browns were playing at Houston, clinging to a 17–14 lead in a late-season game for the AFC Central Division lead. The Oilers were driving late. All day long, Ken Stabler had been going to Dave Casper and burning the Browns on third down, sometimes on second down. The Browns had excellent coverage but had no answer for it. "On that late drive, I think Stabler had gone to Casper twice already," King said. "Well, the third time, Scott read it, stepped in front of Casper, and made the interception, clinching the win. That was Clarence Scott at his best, reading and reading and back there playing possum, and all of a sudden he makes the play that needed to be made."

"Maybe he wasn't the most physically gifted guy, but he knew where the ball was coming," Jeff Schudel said. "The

Joe Haden (JERRY COLI/DREAMSTIME.COM)

number of interceptions he had is reflective of his anticipation and knowledge of where things were going."

"Clarence was the old man of those guys back there when I was there," said Joe DeLamielleure. "He was a real leader and real smart. He could get to the ball and was ferocious. Everybody looked up to him."

The Browns missed on several draft picks when Butch Davis was the head coach in the early 2000s, but they didn't miss on **Anthony Henry**. "Henry was athletic and made tremendous leaps," said King. "He was a great player. He stepped right in from the get-go. His rookie season was very good. He had a nose for the football. He was a guy who, if the ball was up in the air, was going to go get it. He was a special player."

"Obviously, you get that many interceptions, you're a smart player because you have a nose for the football," Dieken said.

"Henry was one of those big guys for a cornerback," said Mike McLain. "I thought he was going to be a great player, but he really only had that one great year."

"He was like a flash in the pan but a big flash," Schudel added. "He was fast and had good hands."

The Browns should have never cut **Joe Haden**, according to Schudel.

"Haden was a cocky guy, confident, and he was a leader on the team by his words and actions, too," he said.

"He was a great player on a team that wasn't playing well," said King. "For the first four or five years of his career, he was a very good cornerback. He was his harshest critic. He was hard on himself, would blame himself for things. He was a standup guy."

"Joe became a very good player but wasn't dependable because of injuries," said McLain.

SAFETIES

Ken Konz
Ross Fichtner
Mike Howell
Thom Darden
Eric Turner

Ken Konz played mostly left safety for the Browns from 1953 to 1959. He amassed 30 career interceptions with a high of seven in 1954. He had five interceptions in both 1953 and 1955. He returned four interceptions for touchdowns. He had two pick-sixes in 1954—a 25-yarder in a 34–14 victory over Washington on December 5 and a 54-yarder in a 42–7 rout of Pittsburgh the very next week on December 12. He returned an interception 15 yards for a touchdown in a 41–14 triumph over the Steelers on November 20, 1955. His last pick-six was a 46-yarder in a 21–17 loss to the Giants on November 2, 1958. Konz was a Pro Bowler in 1955.

Ross Fichtner played both left safety and right safety for the Browns from 1960 to 1967. He totaled 27 interceptions in his career, three of which were returned for touchdowns. He returned an interception 36 yards for a touchdown in a 27–17 win over the Cowboys on November 24, 1963. He returned an interception 32 yards for a score in a 35–17 victory over Philadelphia on October 3, 1965. He had a 39-yard pick-six in a 33–21 loss to the Eagles on December 11, 1966.

Playing left safety and right safety for Cleveland from 1963 to 1965, Larry Benz had 16 career interceptions—seven in 1963, four in 1964, and five in 1965. He was a solid player who seems to get overlooked when the subject is talented Browns players of the past.

After spending his first few seasons as a right cornerback, Mike Howell was a safety for the rest of his career with the Browns, which lasted from 1965 to 1972. He played free safety and right safety. He totaled 27 career interceptions with a high of eight in 1966. He had six picks in both 1968 and 1969.

Ernie Kellerman was a left safety for most of his Browns career, which lasted from 1966 to 1971. He had 17 career interceptions with the Browns with a high of six in 1968, his lone Pro Bowl season. He returned an interception 40 yards for a touchdown in a 20–7 win over Green Bay on December 7, 1969.

Thom Darden played mostly free safety for Cleveland from 1972 to 1974 and 1976 to 1981. His 45 career interceptions are a Browns record. He had an NFL-leading 10 picks in 1978 (his only Pro Bowl year), eight picks in 1974, seven picks in 1976, and six picks in 1977. He returned two interceptions for touchdowns—an 18-yarder in a 44–7 rout of the Chiefs on October 30, 1977, and a 39-yarder that broke Roger Staubach's string of 154 consecutive passes without a theft dating back to the previous season in a 26–7 defeat of Dallas on September 24, 1979. He returned a fumble 29 yards for a score in a 21–14 win over the Patriots on November 10, 1974.

Playing strong safety and free safety for the Browns from 1985 to 1990 was Felix Wright. Wright had 26 career interceptions with the team with a high—and an NFL-best—of nine in 1989. He returned two interceptions for touchdowns—a

40-yarder (he had two picks in the game) in a 30–17 Monday night victory over the Rams on October 26, 1987, and a 27-yarder in a 42–31 win over Tampa Bay on November 5, 1989.

Eric Turner played free safety and strong safety for the Browns from 1991 to 1995. He had 17 career interceptions for Cleveland with a high of—and league-leading—nine in 1994, his only First-Team-All-Pro and Pro Bowl year. He had two pick-sixes with the Browns—a 42-yarder in a 32–30 loss to the Eagles on November 10, 1991, and a 93-yarder (he had two picks in the game) in a 32–0 rout of Arizona on September 18, 1994.

Players in the running to be the Browns' best ever safeties are Konz, Fichtner, Howell, Darden, and Turner.

KEN KONZ

Ken Konz was a feisty player. He wasn't afraid to tell you he was good.

"He had a little bit of a swag about him," said Steve King. "He was a big part of those Browns' defenses in the '50s that were great but got overshadowed by the offense."

"Kenny was a good ballplayer," Jim Ray Smith said.

ROSS FICHTNER

Ross Fichtner was a ball-hawk, that's for sure.

"He could run with the ball pretty well, too," said Mike Peticca.

Fichtner was undersized but very disciplined in terms of understanding what he had to do at his position. He dedicated himself to being the safety valve, making sure opposing teams could not throw the football successfully deep in the middle of the field. Said Paul Warfield, "He never disregarded what his responsibilities were and fit into our scheme of coverage to how he was asked to play."

A favorite of Blanton Collier, Fichtner was a good, solid defensive back. "He wasn't a guy who physically was going to wow you," Steve King said, "but his ability to position himself in terms of being able to make the play and studying and reading helped those Browns defenses."

"Ross was a leader back there in the defensive backfield," added Fred Hoaglin. "He was a good tackler, a tough guy, and he was smart."

"It was a real honor to be able to play pro football," Fichtner said. "I'm so thankful I was a Cleveland Brown. Cleveland was a great place to play. The Cleveland fans were great. And that old stadium . . . I loved playing in it. For teams that came out of that dugout and looked at that big, old monster, I think it was very intimidating with all the fans and stuff even though they were a mile away. And especially with the Browns' records at that time when they were beating people quite regularly, it had to be very, very, very awesome to walk up and step out on to that field. That stadium . . . I think that was part of the magic."

MIKE HOWELL

Mike Howell was very athletic and was a hard hitter, a very aggressive player.

"He was a great interceptor, too," said Steve King. "Every year but two in his time with the Browns, they made the playoffs, and he was a big reason for that."

Howell was also an outstanding cover guy. "He had as good of cover skills as anybody who I ever saw play with the Browns," John Wooten said. "He had instincts for the ball."

"He was a very, very talented player," Paul Warfield said.

THOM DARDEN

Thom Darden played his position very well. His interceptions total proves that.

"In the mold of a Ross Fichtner, it was very difficult to move Thom out of the center of the field," said Paul Warfield. "I thought he brought certainly a lot of intellect to the position. He understood what his job was. In addition to that, he posed another issue for receivers in that he developed into a pretty good big hitter in the secondary. I have respect for Thom. I thought he did a very good job. When he was there, the Browns were not necessarily hurt with deep post patterns. He proved to be a very solid and strong tackler, too."

Darden had great range in pass coverage, had good hands, and was a big hitter. Most Browns teams have not had the reputation of having big hitters, but Darden was one of those guys who stood out within a Browns context as an intimidator. "He had a nose for the ball," said Mike Peticca. "If you were a Browns fan, he was another one of those guys you didn't have to worry about. He was usually going to be better than the guys he was going against, almost always. He was really good."

A knee injury caused Darden to miss the entire 1975 season. "Because I was out in '75, I was just ready to play the next year," he said. "That's when I started really becoming a pretty decent player on the pro level."

Those were high standards considering he had eight interceptions in 1974. "I felt I was getting better," he said, "because of my work ethic and feeling more comfortable with what I was supposed to be doing and making the adjustments. I had to make all the adjustment calls for the linebackers and secondary. I was sort of like the quarterback on the defense."

Darden's return of a Roger Staubach pass 39 yards for a touchdown gave the Browns a 20–0 lead over visiting Dallas— "America's Team"—before the Cowboys had gained even a single first down en route to a 26–7 upset win on *Monday Night Football* on September 24, 1979, which upped the Browns' record to 4-0. "That place was rockin'!" declared Darden. "The electricity in the stadium that night was unbelievable. It was certainly one of my finer moments."

"Thom was good," said Mike Pruitt. "You threw that ball in the wrong direction, he was gonna get it. He was really the leader on the defense. He called a lot of the shots in the defensive backfield. We called him the 'traffic cop' because he'd be directing people where to go on defense."

"Thom was an excellent player," Ray Yannucci said. "He was a talented guy, a very smart guy."

ERIC TURNER
Eric Turner was a hard hitter.

"Turner was a great hitter, a great player in terms of having a nose for the ball," said Steve King. "He was very athletic. He was a very, very good player."

"Eric would come up and smoke you," said Doug Dieken.

"He was probably the hardest hitting safety during his era," Ray Yannucci added. "He was a tough, hard-hitting guy."

"I remember him making a game-saving tackle on Dallas's Jay Novacek in 1994 at Dallas," said Mike McLain.

AND THE WINNERS ARE . . .
The fact that **Thom Darden** has the most interceptions of any player in Browns history is enough to award him one of the spots as one of the best Browns safeties of all time. He was also a fearsome hitter. Wide receivers had to think twice before going across the middle to catch a pass with Darden lurking in the defensive backfield.

Ken Konz does not have the amount of interceptions that Darden has, but he played in two fewer seasons than Darden did. Konz had a pretty large number of picks himself. With Eric Turner right behind him, he deserves the other spot as one of the greatest Browns safeties of all time.

SAFETIES WHO DID NOT MAKE THE CUT

Larry Benz went undrafted but was contacted by both the Browns and the American Football League's Broncos.

"I thought, 'You know what? I love the Browns. I'm gonna go there, I'm gonna get cut,'" recalled Benz, who had spent much of his childhood living in Cleveland. "I had time to get cut and then go to Denver. I just thought that's how it would play out."

At the Browns' tryout, there were a dozen other players— All-Americans who were bigger and faster than Benz. "I was really fortunate, though," he said. "I came to a good, organized team. If you were a smart kid and were always in the right position, they realized that. Other kids were bigger, faster . . . but I always graded out well whenever they reviewed the film."

He chose the Browns over the Broncos even though Denver offered much more money.

"Otto Graham and some of the other Browns would come to talk to our team when I was in high school," said Benz. "I never thought that I, one day, would be playing for the Browns! And . . . I got to play with Jim Brown, the greatest athlete I've ever seen by far."

"Before I even signed my contract," Benz said, "Bernie Parrish called me and we started working out together. He gave me all the tips that a veteran has to help a rookie out."

Benz was a little bit undersized, but in the deep middle against long passes he was always where he needed to be and made sure that things happened in front of him and not behind him and over his head. "What was impressive about the free safety in the Paul Brown-Blanton Collier era," said Paul

Warfield, "was that they were highly disciplined, they were protective of the deep middle more so than making plays up in front of them and tackling people. They were highly disciplined and did their jobs."

"Benz knew the game and knew where he was supposed to be," said Tom Melody. "He certainly made the most, and then some, of the talent that God gave him."

"Larry was a tough, little guy," John Wooten said. "He was smart, a good hitter, had a good nose for the football. He played strong for us. He did a good job."

Ernie Kellerman was not exactly a great physical specimen but was a very smart player, a very good player.

"Ernie was what you call a strong-side safety devoted to mainly defending against tight ends," said Warfield. "He was

Felix Wright with the football against the Broncos
(JERRY COLI/DREAMSTIME.COM)

undersized a little bit, but that did not hamper him. He showed unusual toughness for a man his size. He developed into a very good coverage man."

"Ernie was a tough, hardnosed player," Fred Hoaglin said. "He was a big guy. He hit guys really hard."

Felix Wright probably overachieved. He wasn't in the mold of a Thom Darden or Eric Turner, but he was a very dependable player.

"Felix was a really good player," said Mike Peticca. "He was smart, he had good range, I thought he made a lot of big-game plays. Not necessarily an interception, not necessarily on a blitz, but he just wouldn't miss a tackle late in the game. He was a really reliable tackler with a combination of his speed and range. He was underrated as a hitter."

"He was a great safety, was a hard hitter, was smart, and had great hands," said Steve King.

"He made a lot out of his talents by being in the right place at the right time," Doug Dieken said.

SPECIAL TEAMS

KICKER

Lou Groza
Don Cockroft
Phil Dawson

There is a reason that Lou Groza was nicknamed "The Toe." He was the ultimate clutch kicker. Perhaps the most famous field goal he ever made was his 16-yarder late in the game that gave the Browns a 30–28 comeback victory over the Los Angeles Rams in the 1950 NFL championship contest. A week earlier, he booted the game-winning 28-yard field goal with less than a minute to play in Cleveland's 8–3 playoff win over the New York Giants. The week before that, in the regular-season finale, he broke a 24-year-old NFL record by kicking his 13th field goal of the season.

Groza also kicked some very long field goals, such as his 51-yarder against the Chicago Rockets on November 17, 1946. Two years later, in the season opener against the Los Angeles Dons, he repeated his feat by booting another 51-yard trey. Five weeks later, on October 10, he was successful on a 53-yarder against the Brooklyn Dodgers that was then the longest in pro football history. In the 1951 NFL title game against the Rams, he kicked a 52-yard field goal, a record for an NFL championship game or Super Bowl that stood for 42 years. He booted another 52-yarder against the Giants on October 12, 1952. The next season, he made 23 of 26 field goal tries for an 88.5 percent success rate, an NFL record that stood for 28 years. He kicked 51-yard field goals against the Chicago Cardinals on December 16, 1956, and the Pittsburgh Steelers on October 28, 1962.

Don Cockroft will always be remembered for a kick he never got the chance to try. With the Browns easily within field goal range and down by two points with less than a minute to go in an AFC divisional playoff against Oakland in polar conditions on January 4, 1981, Sam Rutigliano decided to try a pass into the end zone. Brian Sipe was intercepted, and the Kardiac Kids were dead. It is too bad that Cockroft is known more for that than anything else, because he had a very good career with Cleveland from 1968 to 1980. He led the NFL in field goal percentage in his rookie season of 1968, in 1972, and in 1974. In 1972, he won *Pro Football Weekly*'s Golden Toe Award.

Matt Bahr was one tough cookie. On kickoff returns, he didn't just stand around and wait for one of his teammates to make the tackle. He looked to make the tackle himself. That aggressive attitude landed him on the injured list when he hurt himself while trying to make a tackle on a kickoff return against Pittsburgh on November 23, 1986. Bahr happened to be a very fine kicker, too. He came to Cleveland during the early part of the 1981 season in a trade with San Francisco. He had a so-so '81 campaign with the Browns and a terrible 1982 season. Rutigliano, however, had faith in him, and that faith paid off. Bahr led the entire NFL the next season with an 87.5 percent success rate on field goals. He was a very good kicker in his days with Cleveland, which lasted through 1989. He was successful on several crucial field goal tries.

Seemingly forgotten by many Browns fans, Matt Stover had a pretty darned good five seasons with Cleveland from 1991 to 1995. He led the league in 1994 with a 92.9 percent success rate on field goals [26-of-28]. The next year, he made good on 29 of 33 field goal tries for an 87.9 percent success rate.

Matt Stover (Jerry Coli/Dreamstime.com)

When Phil Dawson came to Cleveland in 1999, no one knew who he was. On November 14 of that 1999 season, people knew who he was. That was the day he hurried on to the field and kicked a 39-yard field goal as time ran out that gave the expansion Browns a 16–15 upset of the Steelers in Three Rivers Stadium. Dawson played mainly on bad Browns teams through his last season with the club in 2012, his lone Pro Bowl year. His field goal success rate overall with the Browns was 84 percent. Twice, he topped 90 percent—93.5 percent in 2012 and 93.1 percent in 2005.

In the running for the greatest Browns kicker ever are Groza, Cockroft, and Dawson.

LOU GROZA

When Lou Groza was the Browns' field goal kicker, the average success rate of kickers was not nearly as high as it is nowadays.

"During those days, sometimes a kicker made less than 50 percent of his field goal attempts," said Mike Peticca. "You knew the Browns were lucky that Groza wasn't that type of guy—you thought of him as the all-time best. Even as he got beyond 40 years old, you figured he had as much of a chance to make a kick as anyone in the sport. He was a fan favorite because he'd made a ton of field goals in the clutch. But they rooted for him just as much because of his longtime identity with Cleveland and all of Ohio, and in part, too, as he got older, because he was persevering and succeeding despite his age, and despite not exactly being a streamlined athlete anymore. And what was really cool, and was never a surprise when it happened, was when he was in on a tackle on one of his kickoffs."

Groza was the NFL's first "name" kicker. When he first came to Cleveland, he caused a sensation right off the bat. "By today's standards, he was not that fantastic a kicker, but in those days he was acknowledged as the best kicker in pro football,"

Bob Dolgan said. "And he didn't want to be just a kicker, he wanted to be a football player. When he kicked off, it wasn't like the kickers do today; they stand back and let somebody else make the tackle. When he kicked off, he led the charge down the field to get that ball carrier."

Groza could be called the father of modern kicking. That is why the kicking award in college is called the Lou Groza Award. It is not the Jan Stenerud Award or any of those other great kickers in league history. They were all great kickers, but Groza was the guy who popularized, and stressed the importance of, the kicking game.

"He made kicking cool," said Steve King. "You talked to Lou Groza and he said he was a left tackle who kicked. A lot of people would say he was a kicker who played left tackle. He was a very good left tackle, a tremendous player. Had he been just a left tackle, he would've been in the Hall of Fame. Had he been just a kicker, he would've been in the Hall of Fame. No one had really put importance on the kicking game and used it as a weapon until Groza came along. He was a tremendous kicker. That guy was money. When the Browns needed him to make a kick, he made it. He was bigger than life. Lou Groza Boulevard didn't get named that way by accident. You talk with Phil Dawson about Groza. He'd get embarrassed when he'd approach one of Groza's records when we got after him about it. He'd say, 'I'm humiliated, I'm embarrassed that my name would be in the same sentence with Lou Groza's.' That's how much respect kickers had for Groza."

"Lou was the greatest there ever was," said Fred Hoaglin. "If we needed to score at the end of the game to win the game, then Lou would be at around the 40-yard line of the opponent. As the offense was moving the ball I'm sure he was thinking, 'I hope they can't make a first down past the 40 so I can kick a long field goal to win this game.' If we got a first down at the 30

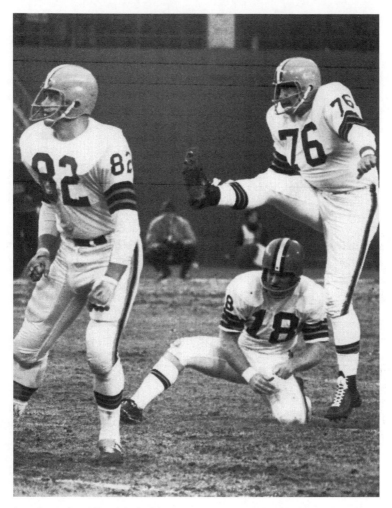

Lou Groza in action late in his career (PAUL TEPLEY/CLEVELAND STATE
UNIVERSITY CLEVELAND PRESS ARCHIVES)

or something like that, you could see Lou with his head down
kicking dirt over on the sideline because he'd know it was going
to be a short field goal or maybe that we were going to score a
touchdown! He was a tremendous competitor.

"At rookie training camp, you'd have a bunch of kickers there. After practice was over was when the kickers would practice. So I would go snap, and the holder would hold, and the kickers would kick. I'd ask the kickers where they wanted to start, and they said, 'Put the ball on the extra point line and we'll kick a few of those and then we'll move back.' When the next week came and the veterans were there, after practice we'd ask Lou where he wanted to start, and he said, 'Put the ball on the 40-yard line. We'll start from there.' And all these young kickers who were trying to get his job, they immediately started shaking. You could see it. Lou knew how to psyche them out."

"I was the holder for Lou for two years," Jim Ninowski, a Browns quarterback in 1958 and 1959 and from 1962 to 1966, said. "He was a great kicker, a pressure kicker."

"From my very first Browns game in 1967, I understood the importance of Lou Groza, and I got to see him kick at a number of games," said longtime Browns fan Fred Zumpano. "He was that link back to the founding of the Browns, to Paul Brown, to my dad's championship Browns. That was a real treat, to be able to see Lou Groza play."

DON COCKROFT

It was the second to last Browns preseason game, at home, in 1968, and Don Cockroft was trying to beat out Lou Groza for the team's kicking position.

"We were playing the Packers in the second game of a doubleheader," said Cockroft. "It was a beautiful, beautiful night. And 80-some thousand [84,918] fans were there. I remember standing on the sidelines looking across that field, and there were Vince Lombardi and Bart Starr.... [Vince Lombardi was Green Bay's general manager in 1968.] I mean, I just got goose bumps standing there during the national anthem, realizing where I was and the opportunity I had. I was so scared and nervous."

Cockroft overcame his jitters and kicked three field goals. "We got beat, 31-9," he said, "but I was the happiest guy in Cleveland." He had made the team, realizing after celebrating five minutes or so, "I'm the kicker for the Cleveland Browns!"

How much pressure did Cockroft feel when he replaced Groza?

"Not to discredit Lou Groza, but I never gave it any thought," he said in the October 2005 *Bernie's Insiders*. "I was so far removed from the professional football scene. We watched pro ball in high school and college, but I was more scared about being in Cleveland, Ohio, trying to make a professional football team more than I was concerned about filling Lou Groza's shoes. There was so much mental anguish, fear, hope, and excitement as it was. I never gave any thoughts about who I was replacing."

When Cockroft, a straight-on kicker, came into the NFL, there were only two soccer-style kickers in the league. "When I left the league, Mark Moseley was the only straight-on kicker left," he said in the October 2005 *Bernie's Insiders*. "So during the years I played was the time when we saw that transition. Soccer kicking when I came in was just beginning, and I didn't even try it until late in my career. I could kick it soccer style, but I had a hard time getting it up off the ground, especially on longer kicks. But I never thought about changing my style."

Municipal Stadium was not exactly a haven for kickers when Cockroft played.

"Let's put it this way," he said. "Every time Jan Stenerud and Garo Yepremian walked into that stadium, they just shook their heads and said, 'I don't know how you kick in this place.' And when Tom Skladany was drafted by the Browns out of Ohio State in 1977, there were rumors that he refused to play in Cleveland because of typical field conditions when it would rain or snow."

"For that era," said Mike Peticca, "Cockroft was absolutely one of the best kickers in the NFL. You could count on him as much as virtually any kicker in the league. Everybody had their big misses in those days . . . Stenerud, Yepremian. They all missed big kicks. But, in those days, if you made two-thirds of your kicks, you were doing really well. Cockroft had good range. People look at the '80 season. Well, he was hurt all year. He had multiple injuries. That had to be a big reason for how the play-off game against Oakland played out as it did. If Cockroft had been healthy, you might not have seen the Browns passing from the 13-yard line. I think he was maybe as much of a team leader as a place kicker/punter can be."

Perhaps Cockroft's most memorable field goal came at home in a crucial game against Pittsburgh on November 19, 1972. With the Browns trailing, 24–23, late in the game, Cockroft was sent on to attempt a 27-yard field goal.

"I never prayed so hard in my life," he said. "It was a muddy, nasty field that day, but basically the snap and hold were good. I kicked the ball, and I pulled up, looked up too quick. I wanted to see it go through the uprights. That ball missed by about two inches to the right. And only the Pittsburgh Steelers were yelling and screaming. The rest of that stadium was dead silent. It was the most devastating moment of my career because it was such an important kick."

Cockroft returned to the sideline with his head down. "Billy Andrews came over and said, 'Don, get your chin up,'" recalled Cockroft. "We're gonna get the ball back. We're gonna give you a second chance."

The Browns did get the ball back.

"I think Nick Roman and Jerry Sherk sacked Terry Bradshaw on third down," Cockroft remembered. "And, if I'm not mistaken, Leroy Kelly returned the punt to about the 50. There were about two minutes left. I knew if we could get a couple first downs, I'd get a second chance. I literally prayed, 'God, I'll keep my head down, please give me a second chance.' Now, I realize there are Christians on both sides of the ball, but all I know is, I got that second chance."

Cockroft was sent on to the field with 13 seconds left. "Unbelievably," he said, "the ball was within inches of where it was before when I missed."

This time, Cockroft kept his head down.

"I drove the ball and, before I looked up, I said, 'It's gotta be good!'" he remembered. "I tell people I saw heaven that day because that sucker sailed dead center through the uprights."

The Browns won, 26–24.

"Don was an excellent kicker," said Fred Hoaglin. "He really did his job well."

PHIL DAWSON

Playing for a losing team can take its toll.

Not for Phil Dawson.

Dawson was on many, many poor Browns teams during his career with Cleveland.

"When you sign your name on the contract, you say you are going to do your job," he said in the February 2005 *Bernie's Insiders.* "It doesn't say 'if the team is winning' or 'if the team is headed in the right direction.' It says, 'Phil Dawson, it is your job to go out and kick the football.' None of the other stuff matters. As a competitor, you want to reach certain achievements each year, and each year that you fail to reach those achievements it becomes harder to take."

Dawson was as good as any kicker in the league at the time he played. Nobody with the "new" Browns has understood the old Browns better than him. "When he kicked the winning field goal as time ran out to beat Pittsburgh in 1999, he was celebrating with his teammates but was pretty blasé about it,"

Steve King said. "His dad got him on the phone and said, 'You know what you've done?' Dawson said, 'Well, I kicked the field goal to win the game.' And his dad said, 'You beat the Pittsburgh Steelers!' It was then that Dawson started learning about the history of the Browns. By the end of his Browns career, he

Phil Dawson kicking against the Ravens (JERRY COLI/DREAMSTIME.COM)

knew about Lou Groza, he knew about the wind currents in the stadium and how they were different from the wind currents in the old stadium. Regarding his two field goals against Buffalo in '07 [in a terrible weather game], you will never in your life see field goals uncannier than those."

"On one of those kicks in the Bills game, the wind was so bad he kicked the ball aiming for the front left corner of the end zone, and the ball went through the goalpost," remembered Jeff Schudel. "The wind was so bad, the snow was so bad, but he came through."

"Those two field goals he had against Buffalo were maybe combined as a pair in one game the best in the history of the NFL," said Mike McLain. "Those two field goals were unmatched in league history under those conditions."

"I'm not a big fan of kickers, but I'm a big fan of Phil Dawson," Doug Dieken said. "He played offensive tackle when he was in grade school, so he was tough. He'd make tackles on kickoff returns and things like that. He's a first-class guy. For me to like a kicker, it takes a lot."

And the Winner Is . . .

Lou Groza, in his time, was as good as any kicker in the NFL. His career field goal percentage is much lower than Phil Dawson's and Don Cockroft's, but for his era, he was money in clutch situations, and the Browns had many clutch situations while Groza was their kicker.

Cockroft was also very good when it came to crucial field goal attempts. He had a handful of seasons that were below par, but overall he was one of the best kickers in team history.

Dawson's problem was that he played for teams that, the majority of the time, were pitiful, so there were far fewer clutch situations in which he kicked. He just didn't have as many opportunities as Groza and Cockroft did to win games at the end because the Browns were losing big most of the time.

In a close race, we go with **Lou Groza** as the Browns' all-time greatest kicker.

KICKERS WHO DID NOT MAKE THE CUT

Matt Bahr had a relatively slow start to his career as a kicker in 1979 and 1980 with Pittsburgh, the start of the 1981 season with San Francisco, and his first two seasons with the Browns. But, beginning in 1983, he really came into his own and performed well.

"When the Browns needed a kick during the '80s, Bahr was money," said Steve King. "He provided the Browns with what they needed when a drive would stall. Getting him in a trade with the 49ers was one of the best moves the Browns have ever made."

Bahr made a lot of crucial kicks. "He obviously was mentally tough because he made so many big kicks," Mike Peticca said. "I can't remember that there was ever a question that anybody was concerned that Bahr at least mentally wasn't going to be equal to the task. He was a guy who you'd want out there with the game on the line.

"I think, every once in a while, he lifted the whole team and inspired the whole team because he was a tough guy as far as getting into the play and making a tackle here and there."

"He was underrated, a very good kicker," said Mike McLain.

"If he'd been 100 pounds bigger and a foot taller, he'd have been a hell of a football player. That's how tough he was. Tough and aggressive," said Ray Yannucci. "He *looked* to tackle people on kickoffs."

With **Matt Stover**, the Browns were very solid in the kicking department in the early 1990s.

"The Browns needed a kicker because they'd cut Bahr at the end of training camp in 1990, replacing him with Jerry Kauric," King recalled. "And Bill Belichick had known Stover since he'd been drafted by the Giants in 1990."

"Stover was one of the best kickers the Browns have ever had," said Yannucci. "He was one of the best kickers of all time."

KICK RETURNER

THE CANDIDATES

Bobby Mitchell
Leroy Kelly
Gerald McNeil
Eric Metcalf
Josh Cribbs

A fabulous kick returner for the Browns from 1958 to 1961, Bobby Mitchell had three punt returns for touchdowns and three kickoff returns for touchdowns with Cleveland. His longest kickoff return was for 98 yards—the first score of the game—in a 28–14 victory over the Eagles on November 23, 1958. His longest punt return went for 78 yards and a touchdown in a 48–7 loss to the Giants on December 6, 1959. Mitchell averaged almost 27 yards per kickoff return in 1961.

Leroy Kelly was a kick returner for Cleveland mostly in the early part of his career. He returned one punt for a touchdown in 1964 and two in 1965. He had a 68-yard punt return for a touchdown that gave the Browns the lead for good in a 42–20 victory over the Giants on October 25, 1964. He had a 67-yard punt return for a touchdown in a 24–17 win over Dallas on November 21, 1965. The very next week, on November 28, he returned a punt 56 yards for the first score of the game in a 42–21 win over the Steelers. His longest punt return went for 74 yards in a 27–0 loss to Denver on October 24, 1971. He averaged 19 yards per punt return in 1964 and 25.9 yards per kickoff return in 1965.

Ben Davis was a kick returner for Cleveland for only two seasons, in 1967 and 1968, but he was a very good one. He averaged 12.7 yards per punt return in 1967. Included was a 52-yard return for a touchdown in a 34–14 triumph over Pittsburgh on November 5. He averaged 26.2 yards per kickoff return in 1967, including a long of 63 yards.

A kick returner for the Browns from 1979 to 1983, Dino Hall was only 5-foot-7, 165 pounds, but he played much bigger than that. He averaged 10.2 yards per punt return in 1979, including a 47-yarder. He averaged 22.6 yards per kickoff return in 1981, including a 48-yarder.

In tiny Gerald McNeil, who was 20 pounds lighter than Hall, the Browns had a guy who was so small that tacklers had a hard time finding him! In 1986, his rookie season, he had returns for touchdowns in consecutive weeks. On September 28, he returned a punt 84 yards for a touchdown in a 24–21 victory over the Lions. The very next week, on October 5, he returned a kickoff 100 yards for a score in a 27–24 win over Pittsburgh. McNeil averaged 11.4 yards per punt return in 1987 and 21.2 yards per kickoff return in 1986. He was a Pro Bowler in 1987.

Eric Metcalf was pure excitement. He had five punt returns for touchdowns and two kickoff returns for scores during his Browns career that lasted from 1989 to 1994. The signature game of his career came on October 24, 1993, in a 28–23 home win over the Steelers. He returned two punts for touchdowns that day—for 91 and 75 yards. The 75-yarder occurred late in the fourth quarter with the Browns down by two points and turned out to be the game-winning score. Metcalf returned a kickoff 90 yards for a touchdown in a 34–30 win over Buffalo in an AFC divisional playoff on January 6, 1990.

Hanging up Hall of Fame numbers with the Browns from 2005 to 2012, Josh Cribbs had eight kickoff returns for touchdowns and three punt returns for scores. He was a threat to go all the way whenever he touched the ball. He returned three

Josh Cribbs in action (JERRY COLI/DREAMSTIME.COM)

kickoffs for touchdowns in 2009 alone! Two of them were in the same game, actually the same half [first]!—100- and 103-yarders in a 41–34 triumph at Kansas City on December 20. He averaged 13.5 yards per punt return and an incredible 30.7 yards per kickoff return in 2007. He was First-Team All-Pro in 2009 and was picked for the Pro Bowl in 2007, 2009, and 2012.

The players in the running for best Browns kick returner ever are Mitchell, Kelly, McNeil, Metcalf, and Cribbs.

BOBBY MITCHELL

Bobby Mitchell was a sensational kick returner.

"Mitchell was as quick and as elusive and as fast and as un-tackleable as any guy in the league," said Steve King.

"Bobby had outstanding punt and kickoff return abilities," John Wooten said. "He had great speed."

LEROY KELLY

From his very first season, it was obvious that Leroy Kelly was something special in the return game.

"Leroy Kelly and Walter Roberts, too, both of whom were rookies along with me, combined to be two of the most danger-ous return men on both punts and kickoffs," said Paul Warfield. "They were just phenomenal."

"Leroy and I put our offense in some pretty good field posi-tion," Roberts said proudly.

"You just remember on every kickoff and punt return thinking, 'Hey, this might be a fun play to watch,'" opined Mike Peticca regarding Kelly.

Added Steve King, "He was about as good as it gets."

GERALD MCNEIL

Gerald McNeil's heroics in the Browns' 27–24 win at Pittsburgh on October 5, 1986, just may have been bigger than people might think.

"If McNeil doesn't run the 100-yard kickoff return that day, the Browns don't win that game," said Steve King. "If they don't win that game, the confidence in the Browns to be able to go on and make it all the way to the AFC Championship game maybe doesn't happen. That was a big play."

McNeil was able to get full speed ahead very quickly on his kick returns. "He got into fast gear right away, zero to 60 in two seconds, one second, whatever it was," King said. "Right away, he was lightning quick. After his stutter-step move, he was gone."

"He was very exciting," said Mike Peticca. "The Browns hadn't had that dimension consistently for some time. He was the first guy to provide a consistency there stretching over a number of years. It was more than the consistency because obviously he could break something at any time. Opponents feared him. He was simply so fast and so little, too. It might sound a little silly, but that's not much of a target at that speed. He definitely was an integral part of those late '80s teams."

"McNeil was little, but that didn't stop him. He was fearless," Jeff Schudel added. "He was so slippery and made people miss."

McNeil was listed at 147 pounds. He laughed about that and once said that his weight was actually 125 pounds at the time. "For a guy his size, Gerald was a really, really tough guy because he took some shots, and there wasn't a lot of meat on the bones with him," said Doug Dieken. "He was fun to watch."

"Anybody who plays at that size I give credit for the guts they have," said Mike McLain. "Gerald was always a threat to break it all the way every time he touched the ball."

ERIC METCALF

Eric Metcalf was fast. It's as simple as that.

"He was electric. I don't know of a better word to describe him," said Mike Peticca. "As a punt returner, he fielded the punt in a position where, in your mind you say, 'This isn't really going to go anywhere because we see all the defenders around him.' Well, he'd do something magical and, all of a sudden, he's out of there gone. I don't know how he's remembered around the country or around the league, but he had to be one of the best ever because he could turn nothing into virtually everything with one quick move and a burst."

"Metcalf, in my time covering the Browns, was probably one of the most gifted athletes they've ever had," Ray Yannucci said. "He was super-fast. He had almost Barry Sanders-type moves. He could've been a superstar had he been used properly [from the line of scrimmage]. Paul Warfield always said that you had to put Metcalf in space, not as a set running back. Put him out in space, split him out, put him in a mismatch with a linebacker or a safety, put him on screens, put him on quick throws, stuff like that."

"He got a lot of opposing coaches frustrated on his kick returns," Jeff Schudel added. "He was so fast."

Metcalf admitted that speed is crucial to being a great kick returner—he was once clocked at 4.28 in the 40-yard dash—but said that moves are even more important. "The ability to make the first guy miss is crucial," he said, "because, as a punt returner especially, there are always going to be guys coming down for you. Somebody has to be free, unblocked, so you're going to have to make somebody miss. Just being able to do that is what made me and the Browns successful at it."

He said having good blockers is critical, too. "We had guys on our team who made it easy for us," he said. "We had corner-backs playing on the special teams who could single up the flyer

Eric Metcalf (JERRY COLI/DREAMSTIME.COM)

so we didn't have to double-press all the time. That leaves more guys in the middle to block. The way we ran our schemes made it a lot easier than people would think. If you have a guy, say Devin Hester, back there returning punts, your special teams are thinking, 'We can score every time if we do our part.' So you have that confidence you can score every time with a Hester or whoever is back there. You're going to block harder to spring him."

The attitude of special teamers is important as well, according to Metcalf. "On the other side of the ball," he explained, "you've got people who don't really want to cover kicks. So, if they don't want to cover kicks and they're playing a team that really wants to block for people who can score, it makes it that much easier."

Metcalf was responsible for the last truly thrilling athletic moment in old Cleveland Stadium. "The last time that the fans at the old stadium roared like you remembered all of those years that they roared was the two punt returns for touchdowns by Metcalf against the Steelers in 1993," said Steve King. "You couldn't describe that excitement to anybody unless you were there. They had to be there to really grasp what that was."

"I was down on the field for his second punt-return touchdown of the game," recalled Mike McLain. "To this day, I don't know if I've ever heard a louder stadium. It was incredible. My ears were reverberating. I thought I was going to just kind of fall over."

"It was very exciting," Metcalf said. "I wasn't even supposed to play! I had a sprained knee. I'll never forget that day. I'm glad I could do it and that people will always remember it."

JOSH CRIBBS

Who in their wildest dreams would foresee that a player from Kent State University—Kent State!—would develop into the kind of kick returner that Josh Cribbs did?

"Josh Cribbs was more of a workman-like runner. He ran quickly north and south," said Steve King. "He didn't have all the electricity of a Bobby Mitchell or a Greg Pruitt or an Eric Metcalf, but he didn't waste any energy. He found a hole and went. Had he been on better teams, he would've been seriously considered for the Hall of Fame. I'll never forget that one where he dropped the ball and then dropped it again at Pittsburgh in 2007. You thought, 'Oh my god, they're gonna tackle him in the end zone.' There were guys all around him and, like he's Moses walking on water, he goes for a touchdown. Unbelievable. Unbelievable!"

"If you don't talk about Cribbs as being in the top 10 returners in league history, you're doing him a disservice. He was that good," said Mike McLain. "You didn't want to tackle him when he was breaking away on a return because he'd run you over or run around you."

"He was so big that he could run over people," Jeff Schudel said. "Most kick returners are not his size."

AND THE WINNER IS . . .

Bobby Mitchell was extremely dangerous as a kick returner. Six returns for touchdowns in four seasons as a Brown is enough proof of that. When you kicked the ball to him, anything was possible.

Leroy Kelly is a Hall of Famer because of his talents as a halfback, but he first made a name for himself as a kick returner. And he was a very good one. Any time he touched the ball, he was capable of going all the way.

As for Gerald McNeil, he was so little and so fast. He was a speed demon. He was sensational at evading tacklers. And he had guts to go out on a football field as small as he was and to go against players much bigger than him.

With Eric Metcalf, it was July 4th during football season because he provided so many fireworks. Even when he was not returning kicks for touchdowns, he was still fun to watch because he was giving the Browns' offense good field position due to his extraordinary kick-return abilities.

Josh Cribbs has got be considered one of the greatest kick returners in the history of the NFL. He was not only fast, but he was big enough that he could run over tacklers if running by them wasn't an option. He could do it all.

Josh Cribbs gets our vote as the Browns' greatest kick returner of all time.

Kick Returners Who Did Not Make the Cut

Even though he did not come from a big-name school (Defiance College), **Ben Davis** immediately showed that he belonged with the Browns.

"Ben developed the ability to catch the football as a returner and return the ball on a consistent basis," said Paul Warfield. "He gave our offensive unit desired field position so that we could work to have a successful offensive drive."

"That 52-yard punt return for a touchdown against Pittsburgh my rookie year played a big role in me gaining confidence that I could play in the NFL," Davis said.

"For a short period of time, he was a great kick returner," said Steve King. "He had the ability to run north and south."

Pound for pound, **Dino Hall** may have been one of the toughest football players ever. "Dino was a lot tougher than his size," said Joe DeLamielleure. "He wasn't big, but, man, he was tough."

"Dino might be one of my all-time favorites as a football player," Doug Dieken said. "He wouldn't back down from anybody. I have a picture of the two of us standing side by side on the sidelines, and with his helmet off he didn't even come up to the top of my shoulder pads."

"I don't know how he made it without having his back broken," said Mike McLain. "He was a serviceable guy who could get you some yards when you needed them."

"Sam Rutigliano cut Hall once, and everybody said to him at the time, 'Sam, you made a mistake. You cut Dino Hall,'" recalled King. "Well, as it turns out, Keith Wright gets hurt, so they re-sign Dino Hall. And he proved to be a great returner. He played with great heart. He wasn't the biggest guy in the world, but he knew how to use his size to his advantage. He was so small, there wasn't much player to grab, and he was quick. He could turn his body sideways."

PUNTER

Horace Gillom
Gary Collins
Chris Gardocki

In his 10 seasons with the Browns from 1947 to 1956, Horace
Gillom led the NFL in punting yards average three times—45.5
in 1951, 45.7 in 1952, and 44.7 in 1956. He had a punt of 73
yards, which led the league, in 1952. He punted a ball 80 yards
in 1954, and that led the league too. He had a career punting
yards average of 43.1. He was picked for the Pro Bowl in 1952.

Gary Collins punted for the Browns from 1962 to 1967.
He led the NFL in punting yards average with 46.7 in 1965.
He had a 73-yard punt in 1963, which was the longest in the
league that season. He punted a ball 71 yards in 1965. He had
only two punts blocked in his career. He had a career punting
yards average of 41.

Don Cockroft was a Browns punter from 1968 to 1976. He
averaged 43.2 yards per punt in 1972 and 42.6 yards per punt
in 1970. Twice, he had punts that traveled 71 yards—against
the Oilers on November 22, 1970, and against the Chiefs on
December 2, 1973. He averaged 40.3 yards per punt in his
career.

Manning Cleveland's punting position from 1999 to 2003, Chris Gardocki averaged 45.5 yards per punt in 2000 and 43.8 yards per punt in 1999. He not only never had a punt blocked with the Browns but never had a punt blocked in his entire 15-year career, including stints with the Bears, Colts, and Steelers. In his five seasons with Cleveland, he averaged 43.4 yards per punt.

Dave Zastudil punted for the Browns from 2006 to 2009. He averaged 45.5 yards per punt in 2008, 44.7 yards per punt in 2009, and 44 yards per punt in 2006. He had a 65-yard punt in 2008 and a 64-yard punt in 2007. He had no punts blocked in his four seasons with the Browns. Also in his days with Cleveland, he averaged 44.1 yards per punt.

In the running for greatest Browns punter ever are Gillom, Collins, and Gardocki.

HORACE GILLOM

Horace Gillom was one of the first punting specialists in the history of the NFL. And, boy, could he punt the ball.

"The ball looked like it was shot out of a cannon coming off of his foot," said Steve King.

"Horace kicked the ball 40 yards high and 40 yards down the field. He gave you time to run under it," said Jim Ray Smith, who also played on the punting team.

"He was a tremendous punter," Bob Dolgan said.

GARY COLLINS

Gary Collins was an outstanding punter with a lot of power.

"If we were backed up on our side of the field, Gary seemingly always had the ability to punt the ball and put the opposing team back in their territory," recalled Paul Warfield. "He was very consistent with his punting. I never saw him really shank a punt or even have a bad punt."

"Gary was a really good punter," said Fred Hoaglin. "He was very, very particular. He'd put his hands down near his right hip, and that's where he wanted the ball. When we were practicing, if I didn't put it right in his hands, then he would make no effort to catch the ball. He'd just let it go by. So I had to get it right in his hands every time because he wanted it done right."

"He could hit it, could drive it, could knock it up in the air," John Wooten added. "He got us out of a lot of jams."

Collins was not only a great punter kicking the ball, but he had great hands to field the snaps, which was not always a given in those days. "There were so many special teams mistakes then," said Mike Peticca. "For that era, he was one of the very best."

CHRIS GARDOCKI

The fact that Chris Gardocki never had a punt blocked is a pretty remarkable statistic for as long as he played.

"Gardocki got rid of the ball quickly, and he could place it too," said Jeff Schudel. "He was more than just getting rid of the ball in a hurry. He could place it inside the 20."

Gardocki was as good of a punter as the Browns have ever had. He was able to put the ball in a spot. It was uncanny. He was an unbelievable punter. "In a 2000 game at home against Pittsburgh, [Steelers head coach] Bill Cowher sent linebacker Joey Porter out there to blast Gardocki, take him out of the game, and eliminate that weapon for the Browns," Steve King recalled. "And Porter took a shot at him, but it didn't happen. Gardocki kind of avoided it. And Gardocki came right over to the Pittsburgh bench, got about 10 yards away from Cowher, and flipped him the bird, becoming a cult hero to Browns fans."

And the Winner Is . . .

Horace Gillom was a great, great punter. So was Gary Collins. **Chris Gardocki**, however, was so good at his craft and so consistent. He had a ton of power and great touch as well. The fact that, in a long career, he never had a single punt blocked gives him the nod as the best Browns punter of all time.

Punters Who Did Not Make the Cut

Don Cockroft was not a great punter, but he was a solid, reliable punter.

"He seldom had a terrible punt," said Mike Peticca. "He was never going to kill your field position."

"Don was not necessarily an outstanding power punter per se, although he certainly had the ability to kick the ball on a consistent basis somewhere between 42-43 yards or thereabout," Paul Warfield said. "He was very accurate with his punting. He could place it and put it wherever he wanted."

"Don was probably one of the best dual kickers the NFL has had," said Ray Yannucci.

When he was relieved of his punting duties in 1977, Cockroft thought it was a bad decision. "I believed I could still punt the football," he said. "I hung the ball very, very high. Oakland's Ray Guy was the only punter during my career who I felt could out-punt me."

Dave Zastudil was one of the better punters in the NFL when he played.

"He was needed at that time by the Browns," said Mike McLain.

"Zastudil was a great punter," said Steve King.

THE CLEVELAND BROWNS ALL-TIME ALL-STAR TEAM

Head coach: Paul Brown

OFFENSE
Quarterback: Otto Graham
Fullback: Jim Brown
Halfback: Leroy Kelly
Tackles: Lou Groza, Dick Schafrath
Guards: Gene Hickerson, Jim Ray Smith
Center: Frank Gatski
Tight end: Ozzie Newsome
Wide receivers: Paul Warfield, Dante Lavelli, Gary Collins

DEFENSE
Ends: Len Ford, Bill Glass
Tackles: Jerry Sherk, Walter Johnson
Nose tackle: Bill Willis
Linebackers: Clay Matthews, Walt Michaels, Jim Houston
Cornerbacks: Hanford Dixon, Frank Minnifield
Safeties: Thom Darden, Ken Konz

SPECIAL TEAMS
Kicker: Lou Groza
Kick returner: Josh Cribbs
Punter: Chris Gardocki

SOURCE NOTES

I'd like to thank the many people I have interviewed about the Cleveland Browns over the years. Without them, this book would not have become a reality. They are Dick Ambrose, Billy Andrews, Mike Baab, Walter Beach, Larry Benz, Brian Brennan, Johnny Brewer, Jim Brown, Earnest Byner, Don Cockroft, Gary Collins, Vince Costello, Dan Coughlin, Thom Darden, Ben Davis, Joe DeLamielleure, Doug Dieken, Hanford Dixon, Bob Dolgan, Ross Fichtner, Bobby Franklin, Bob Gain, Bill Glass, Bob Golic, Ernie Green, Jack Gregory, Carl Hairston, Fred Hoaglin, Fair Hooker, Jim Houston, Jim Kanicki, Leroy Kelly, Steve King, Kevin Mack, Mike McLain, Tom Melody, Eric Metcalf, Frank Minnifield, Dick Modzelewski, Bill Nelsen, Ozzie Newsome, Jim Ninowski, Bernie Parrish, Mike Peticca, Milt Plum, Greg Pruitt, Mike Pruitt, Cody Risien, Walter Roberts, Reggie Rucker, Sam Rutigliano, Frank Ryan, Dick Schafrath, Jeff Schudel, Jerry Sherk, Jim Ray Smith, Paul Warfield, Paul Wiggin, John Wooten, Ray Yannucci, and Fred Zumpano.

Other sources I used for the book are:

Periodicals
Bernie's Insiders/The Orange and Brown Report

Books

Brown, Paul, with Jack Clary. *PB: The Paul Brown Story*. New York: Atheneum, 1979.

Videos

NFL Films. *75 Seasons: The Story of the NFL*. Polygram Video, 1994 (via YouTube).

NFL Films. *The Cleveland Browns: Fifty Years of Memories, 1946–1996*. Polygram Video, 1996 (via YouTube).

NFL Films. *The NFL's Great Games—Volume II*. 1990 (via YouTube).

Other various NFL Films videos

Websites

OleMissSports.com

Pro-football-reference.com

ACKNOWLEDGMENTS

I would like to thank Niels Aaboe of Lyons Press for giving me the opportunity to write this book. Without him, it never would have happened. I would also like to thank the many people I've interviewed about the Cleveland Browns over the years, especially Jim Brown, Steve King, and Mike Peticca.

ABOUT THE AUTHOR

Roger Gordon is a freelance writer who has authored eleven sports books—seven on football—including *Blanton's Browns: The Great 1965-69 Cleveland Browns* and *A Century of NFL Football: The All-Time Quiz*. He is a member of the Professional Football Researchers Association. He lives in North Canton, Ohio.